Simple and Daring
Teaching Social Music Improvisation
Facilitation and Flow

James Oshinsky with Mary Knysh

Creating and Sequencing Music Improvisation Experiences for Students and Adults; a vision for integrating Social Music Improvisation into K-12 public school music

(Keywords: experiential education; improvisation pedagogy; music education; improvisation, Social Emotional Learning)

A lot of preparation goes into being ready to be spontaneous. For musicians, we can become skilled improvisers if we have good models and ample experience, the way we learn to be fluent in a language. For teachers, we can use a parallel process – teaching improvisation with spontaneity – if we immerse ourselves in a supportive atmosphere to take risks and learn by doing. This book provides the path, which is both intentional and intuitive.

"It is an odd truth that American schoolchildren come home with original written stories and their own artwork, but not with their own music. This is because our educational system does not nurture musical creativity as it does visual art and literary creativity. Until music teachers have the tools to teach improvising, this giant hole in arts education will likely persist. We propose ways to integrate Social Music Improvisation into mainstream public-school K-12 music programs, and we suggest how to prepare teachers to present improvisation activities that are engaging, interactive, and memorable."

For over 30 years, Jim Oshinsky has been a musical adventurer, immersed in the teachings of great improvisers. He became an ambassador of a type of music that welcomes everyone. In this volume, Jim shares the resources he has gathered, beginning with the open attitude of the improviser to keep things simple and daring. Simple - in the words of the late David Darling, "to be a master of what you can control." Daring - to jump in, start something, and find your playing partners in the spontaneous music. Jim is a Remo-endorsed drum circle facilitator.

Mary Knysh has been the lead teacher of Music for People and Rhythmic Connections for the past three decades, presenting brain-based programs for immersive music internationally. She is an award-winning trainer of music teachers, using the methods described in this book to craft deep learning experiences with seamless sequences of activities. She is an endorser for Rhythm Band, Toca, and Peripole Music.

The book presents suggestions for teaching social music improvisation to children and adults at all levels of ability and experience. There are specific ideas for incorporating improvisation into the common practices of band, orchestra, and chorus in schools. There are dozens of tried-and-true teaching sequences that provide entryways into the world of spontaneous music. And there is a crosswalk between the teaching of Social Music Improvisation and the main tenets of Social Emotional Learning: identity, belonging, and agency. This approach to improvisation allows people to interact in socially beneficial ways while making artful, authentic, and connected spontaneous music, and contributing to lives of attunement and harmony. The book advocates a supportive and encouraging approach to improvising and teaching improvisation, featuring inclusiveness, acceptance, and honest gentle guidance.

Publication information:

Simple and Daring: Teaching Social Music Improvisation Using Facilitation and Flow.
James Oshinsky with Mary Knysh. ©2023 Bundt Pan Publishing. Soft cover, 130 pages.

Available from the authors:
James Oshinsky   PsyDoctorO@optonline.net   www.tinyurl.com/musicd-
Mary Knysh   MaryKnysh@gmail.com   www.music4wellness.com

Simple and Daring

Teaching Social Music Improvisation Facilitation and Flow

James Oshinsky
with Mary Knysh

Creating and Sequencing Social Music Improvisation Experiences for Students and Adults; a vision for integrating Social Music Improvisation into K-12 public school music.

Foreword

"What is this story you are telling?
What wild song is singing itself through you
Listen, in the silence between there is music
In the spaces between there is story
It is the song you and I are living right now
It is the story of the place where we are
It contains the shapes of these old mountains
and the green of the rhododendron leaves.
It's happening right now to your breath,
In your heartbeat, still drumming,
Drumming, drumming the deeper rhythm beneath your cracking words.
It matters what you did this morning, and last Saturday night
And last year
Not because you are important
Because you are in it.
It matters because you're in it,
And it is still moving
We, you and me, we are in this story together
Listen! in the silence between there is music
In the spaces between there is story
Pay attention dear ones,
Pay attention dear ones
You and me,
We are listening each other into being.

Poem from the collection "Picking Clean the Bones" by Sally S. Atkins

Life is an improvisation. We do not have a score to follow, and we are not told when to support someone or when to speak our mind. We figure it out as we go. We learn literacy only after we establish a basis of social communication that begins with one or two sounds. For language, we learn to listen and respond. Why not teach the foundations of music in this way? Through social conversations, spontaneous interactions, starting simply, and daring to dive in.

First and foremost, music teachers are musicians. This book empowers us to impart the subject we love through active engagement in what we love. I use improvisation in voice lessons to help my students become compassionate, accepting, and open lifelong learners who trust in their abilities to problem-solve and work with others. I want them to value themselves and the experiences that make them who they are. I want their music to tell a story worth telling, and I want them to have the musical skills to listen, create, and collaborate. Improvisation is the way.

I was fortunate enough to have Mary Knysh and Jim Oshinsky as my mentors as I went through Music for People's Musicianship and Leadership Program. Mary embodies improvisational flow in her facilitation; Jim articulates and documents these elusive processes with precision and insight. In this volume, we hear from the witness, the facilitator, and the students/players. We are introduced to the main improvisation forms, the facilitator's mindset, and the experiences of the learners as they engage. We are treated to a rare behind-the-scenes view, with examples of artful sequences and transitions, illustrating how the facilitator/teacher drops into a state of flow while guiding the learning process. Through the act of music improvisation students learn how to listen, adapt, and integrate themselves in novel situations with others as they become more comfortable taking on the roles of supporter and leader as needed. Teachers of improvisation are emboldened to listen, adapt, and integrate their accumulated fund of musical experience with their sensitivity to provide lessons at the student's growing edges. Counselors can benefit from the way this Social Music Improvisation approach painlessly offers opportunities for social interaction and personal discovery.

In a supportive environment without fear of "wrong notes" and expectations, we can allow ourselves to return to the state of childlike wonderment and curiosity that brought us to music in the first place. We can plunge into the same processes as the author and immerse ourselves in playing and teaching in ways we might once have feared. It is a fine thing to read and write about music, but deep learning best happens when you are daring enough to jump in and do it!

Irene Feher, D. Mus.
Concordia University
www.Livingyourmusic.com

"Improvisational Transformation" - Betsy Bevan

Preface

This book is about teaching Social Music Improvisation. While you may think you know what improvisation is, we urge you to pause and wait for the examples that will follow. We are not mainly talking about the way jazz, blues, bluegrass, and rock players take an improvised solo over a set of verse-and-chorus chord changes. That is improvisation, for sure, and at the highest levels of musicianship you can hear the conversations and interactions among the players as they rip through runs of notes or grab our emotions with their expressiveness. The problem with this definition of improvisation is that it excludes so many of us from the elite club of improvisers.

Consider instead the way children interact when they pick up instruments for the first time. They explore, they are hungry for experiences, and they quickly learn what actions make a few satisfying or interesting sounds. They alternate between a personal focus and a social focus. As soon as they have even partly mastered a sound, they broadcast it - "look what I can do!" And their playmates engage in sound play along with them, much like a conversation. Along the way, they may discover ways of socially coordinating – taking turns or playing louder when they play simultaneously. They imitate each other, and they employ the interesting timbres or intervals that they have discovered. They may find common rhythms, or they may march to different drummers. This is also improvisation – spontaneous musical play that is both personally expressive and socially interactive.

While intricate improvisations over chord changes can be taught, there is a long tooling up period during which players have to learn the competencies needed to play in tune, in time, and in the "feel" of the piece. However, there is no need to wait so long to introduce students to more basic techniques for improvised musical interactions. That's where this book comes in. We are hoping to remedy an imbalance in arts education. It is an odd truth that American schoolchildren come home with original written stories and their own artwork, but not with their own music. This is because our educational system does not nurture musical creativity as it does visual art and literary creativity. Until music teachers have the tools to teach improvising, this giant hole in arts education will likely persist. We propose ways to integrate Social Music Improvisation into mainstream public-school K-12 music programs, and we suggest how to prepare teachers to present improvisation activities that are engaging, interactive, and memorable.

We will introduce you to a few dozen simple structures for improvising in small and large groups. This includes elementary general music classes, as well as ensembles such as band, orchestra, and chorus. When music improvisation is presented in an open and social context, you will find that it impacts students in ways that go beyond their competence to make music. We offer an approach to music making that requires the students to listen to each other, to imitate and adjust their playing to their peers, to take turns, and to address their fears and joys when making public sounds. If this sounds like Social Emotional Learning, it's because it is. Individual musical expression is a strong carrier for a person's identity, and common rhythms and tonalities are instant ways of experiencing a sense of group belonging. We are moved by our music and the music of others to social interactions even after the music has stopped ringing. Mainly we will be presenting *what* there is to teach in the way of social improvisation, describing the structures that launch explorations and connections, followed by a description of *how* to approach teaching it, either as its own subject or as add-ons to existing music classes and ensembles with authenticity and spontaneity.

What will make it safe to explore making spontaneous and improvised sounds in front of a room full of peers? The answer includes the absence of criticism, and in its place, relentless positivity and encouragement. In improvisation, safety is supported by the celebration of risk-taking and playfulness so we can try something just to see what it sounds like and learn by doing. As much as possible, we will aim for a welcoming and encouraging tone that we hope will come through the pages and disarm any doubts or reluctance you might have to try making your own sounds, and to teach your students in your own unique way.

In Part One, we will present the main techniques of Social Music Improvisation. These are simple structures and activities that have been developed and refined over the past 35 years by the organization Music for People, inspired by the teaching of David Darling, Mary Knysh, and others. They develop high levels of listening, responsiveness, and expressiveness that are associated with mature musicianship. Part Two goes beyond the basics to more nuanced activities emphasizing support roles and interactions among improvising musicians.

Next, in Part Three, we address why we call this "Social Music Improvisation." We provide a crosswalk between our activities and the main concepts of Social Emotional Learning as presented by Scott Edgar and the ArtsEdSEL organization. In his formulation, the main pillars of Social Emotional Learning are Identity, Belonging, and Agency. These translate to self-expression in music, group coordination through attunement and entrainment, and being moved by music into interpersonal action.

The remaining sections describe how to teach this material. We espouse a mindset of constant encouragement, and we emphasize deepening the learning experience by crafting flowing sequences of connected activities. We provide examples of teaching sequences that have worked well, while advocating the use of emergent and spontaneous events as central to teaching improvisation using improvisational methods. We apply this approach to a variety of age groups from kindergarten through high school, and a variety of settings from general music classes to the common ensembles of band, orchestra, and chorus. We also include recorder and ukulele.

We describe the content of a full college class in Social Music Improvisation, designed to prepare music educators to pass these concepts along to new generations of students. And we present models for showcasing social improvisation in smaller segments, in shorter sampler sessions, and in workshops for adults.

Lastly, we provide an annotated bibliography of resources for teaching Social Music Improvisation in percussion, voice, and mixed instrument settings.

The main body of writing reflects the understandings that psychologist James Oshinsky has developed, based on a lifetime as an improvising musician, and as an "ambassador" of Social Music Improvisation when visiting a broad variety of arts organizations. Jim would not have evolved these insights without immersion in a community of colleagues, collaborating on developing the nuts and bolts of social improvisation, and refining the attitude of compassionate listening and guidance needed to present social improvisation effectively. This book was developed through Jim's conversations with Mary Knysh, who has been the main exponent of Social Music Improvisation since she succeeded David Darling as the lead teacher of Music for People. Mary has been generous in sharing her activities and the mindset of leadership that she embodies in her Rhythmic Connections workshops for school-age children, adults, and elders.

Where the journey began – learning from Paul Winter circa 1984.

Table of Contents

Introduction

Teaching Social Music Improvisation Using Facilitation and Flow

Some people like to teach using a script for their classes - they have decided in advance what they will cover, what words they will use, and what experiences they want their students to have. The class can run like a well-rehearsed piece of theater. In contrast, some people like to teach using notes or an outline - they know the material equally well, but perhaps they crave novelty or trust themselves to be more spontaneous in their teaching, using serendipitous events that arise and cannot be predicted.

When the subject matter being taught is improvisation, there is some irony in using a completely scripted approach. It might be more consistent for a teacher of improvisation, teaching students to trust their own abilities to make music spontaneously and interactively, to trust their *own* ability to teach spontaneously and interactively.

Music Education programs at college level most often teach improvisation as a very small portion of their curriculum. They define musicianship mainly as the ability to competently reproduce written music or to use compositional skill to create written music. Improvisation has a proud place in jazz studies, and to some degree in avant-garde or experimental classical music, but instruction in improvisation is often limited to a few courses at the end of undergraduate training. There is nearly no instruction in improvisation pedagogy. This is, in my way of thinking, a serious missed opportunity to capitalize on the social benefits that are associated with learning how to improvise cooperatively and collaboratively in small groups. But without models or experience, how are teachers supposed to fulfill various state curriculum standards to teach students how to improvise?

Beginning in the 1980s, the organization Music for People (MfP), founded by the late cellist David Darling, began offering workshops and leadership classes in small ensemble and large group social improvisation. The initial model was based on chamber music. A quartet of musicians would start with silence, find each other in an open-ended improvisation playing space, and play until they found a natural ending to their common journey. The resulting music reflected both the instrumental skills of the players and their adeptness at finding ways to connect and interact socially, using both mindfulness and fluency. As a result, the approach appealed to musicians from many musical genres, as well as to educators and therapists who valued the social skills gained when learning to play ensemble music in this manner.

Music for People developed a program that sought to develop both improvisation skills in music making and leadership skills in presenting improvisation experiences to a variety of audiences. True to the values of improvisation as a path to great music and positive social connections, often the manner of presenting improvisation content was itself improvisational in large part. MfP trainees were taught to treat teaching sessions as a ground for improvising the means of delivering content, emphasizing flowing sequences of activities, and using the opportunities for teaching moments that presented themselves in unique ways each time. The main content of Music for People workshops has been written about in previously published works by James Oshinsky, Mary Knysh, and Lynn Miller.

The value of improvising extends beyond the jam session. Students who improvise music together look at each other for cues, synchronize their playing, converse in music, and listen deeply for the places their contributions will fit in with their partners. Not surprisingly, this can lead to higher levels of musicianship when the content is the performance of prepared written music, and they are also prepared to live more harmoniously when the music stops.

We hope you will be inspired by this model of teaching and will risk trying these ideas in your own classrooms, studios, and workshops. And please join the Music for People community to experience this approach close to its source (www.musicforpeople.org).

"It is the child that sees the primordial Secret in Nature,
And it is the child in ourselves we return to.
The child within us is Simple and Daring enough
To live the Secret."

- Lao Tzu

"There is Dignity in Risk" – Jack Kreitzer

Music for People Opens Doors...

"MfP teaches the highest levels of musicianship; social connections with playing partners and personal expression at the edges of risk. Where else can you go to access these lessons?"

Dr. Jim Oshinsky, Grad and Creator, Music Doctor Improv Cards Author, Return to Child

GRAD. JIM OSHINSKY

For well over 30 years, I have worked alongside David Darling, Jim Oshinsky, and thousands of adults and children who have joined me on this fascinating journey of Social Music Improvisation. It has always been my belief that the language of music speaks straight from the heart and that it offers each of us a pathway to understanding others and ourselves in a deeper and more meaningful way. It is my hope that you and those that you teach will discover and harness the transformative power that music improvisation offers to all ages and levels of players.

This book will provide you with WHAT we do in Social Music Improvisation, the WHY behind what we do, and HOW we implement this form of music-making with groups of all ages.

It has been both my great honor and joy to collaborate with Jim Oshinsky on this new book. We hope that you benefit from all that we have shared and go on to inspire others with the joy and power of social improvisation!

-   Mary Knysh

Part One -
Improvising Music Socially – An Introduction to Return to Child Principles

At Adelphi University in New York, all Music Education students are required to take one improvisation class prior to graduation. It is offered at the end of the senior year, in the final semester before graduation. I taught this class for over a decade. I had two goals - to give students experience improvising in solo and ensemble formats, and to give them experience leading improvisation activities that would be suitable for a variety of K-12 teaching situations, from general music classes to performing ensembles. My students were very talented, but often had little prior experience with improvisation. They also had a great deal of fear about making wrong or unplanned notes. Not surprising, given their past experience.

The class was taught using a pedagogical approach that emphasized chaining together a few improvisational music experiences in each teaching segment. This flow prolonged and deepened the listening levels and elevated the music making. Through simp e improvisation games and exercises, disguised by their continuity, we were able to progress in cne semester from nervousness to confidence, hosting an all-improvised concert by semester's end. Teaching expressive and interactive improvisation with an emphasis on flow was pioneerec by Music for People founder David Darling in the 1980s and has been ref ned by the MfP teachers who have followed, most notably Mary Knysh. In this series of essays, we will be illuminating both the content of the MfP approach to improvisation and the teaching methods that are used, emphasizing facilitation and flow, using principles of experientia education. We call these techniques Social Music Improvisation because they are fundamentally interactive and arise from the unique and spontaneous contributions of the players. Social Music Improvisation builds trust, strengthens confidence, and includes people at all levels of ability and experience. Music for People's curriculum book is called Return to Child, which captures the importance of playfulness in this approach.

The Basics. Start with percussion and introduce facilitation hand signals.

We generally begin the first classes jamming on percussion instruments. The intent is to establish an atmosphere of "deep fun." Playful on the one hand, and also respectful of having entered "the temple of music" every time we play together. When we start with percussion, I can assess the rhythmic skills and the social skills of each participant. Even though the majority of the students are Music Education or Music Performance majors, it is not a given that the students are adept at spontaneous, unpracticed music-making. I observe them: Can he or she hold a steady beat? Do they interact with each other musically or do they safely stay locked into patterns? Does this student show a hunger to solo and shine? If so, is their need for attention constructive? Which students bond? Which avoid or repel?

With the class engaged in group rhythm, I can begin to model basic drum circle facilitation gestures and interventions. While these gestures originated in the drum circle community (and have been written about extensively by Arthur Hull), they apply to nearly every musical ensemble, especially larger groups. I cue the group that an instruction is coming with an "attention call," in drum circle language. This gesture can be as simple as raising an index finger and getting eye contact around the group. I will show them hand gestures for getting softer and louder, playfully modulating the dynamics of the group while they are playing. I will identify the 360-degree aspects of working in a circle of musicians, since some part of the group might be behind the facilitator if he or she stands in the center. This leads to the concept of "the rest of the circle," namely, those people who are not included in an instruction either by the leader's intention or because they can't see the leader. If I work from the center of the circle, I keep rotating so that all players see my gestures. The larger the group, the higher above my head I may need to gesture so that I can be seen by all and communicate clearly.

Besides gestures for louder and softer, I introduce the "stop cut" and the count down. A stop cut is exactly what it sounds like – it gets the group to stop in unison. The crisper the better. This is worth working on, since the ensemble-ness of the group, their coordination in time, is immediately audible and reinforcing when they stop as one. To prepare the group for a stop cut, I will generally count down from 4 to 1, saying, "4-3-2-and-out!" or something similar. Early on I will take 4 measures to get from 4 to out! Later this can be accelerated to happen within one measure. Sometimes a stop cut ends a teaching segment. Sometimes the group continues to silently mark time and listen for a cue for a coordinated re-entry.

The "and" in "4-3-2-and-out!" is a crucial step. As I count down, I hold 4 or 3 or 2 fingers in the air. When I get to "and," I cross my arms like a baseball umpire preparing to call someone "safe!" I finish that gesture and uncross my arms, dramatically, on the stop cut. Large and anticipatory gestures help a novice group prepare to follow a leader's intentions. When a group can stop in a coordinated way, they experience an instant sense of accomplishment and bonding.

How I get the group started is also simple. I might start a rhythm on a hand drum, on my lap, or on a cowbell and ask the group to join in as they wish. I might count them in so we start simultaneously, using the following phrase: "1,2, let's all play!" This phrase, in 4/4 time, sets a pulse and subdivides the pulse. It imparts verbal content embedded in a nonverbal rhythmic model. Later we will layer in, one person at a time joining the beat.

Sculpting subgroups

After about five minutes or so of group drumming, I might, depending on the size of the group, begin to sculpt the group into smaller ensembles. These could be based on seating location, in which case I would model cutting the group into sections like cutting a pizza, showing who is in which "slice." Or I might sculpt the group by the timbre of the instruments they are playing and designate a group of all the higher-pitched drums, or just the "spice" instruments such as the shakers, claves, and bells. To do this, I need to introduce a "keep playing" gesture, rolling my hands. If I set up a subgroup to keep playing, I can then

Facilitation Hand Gestures

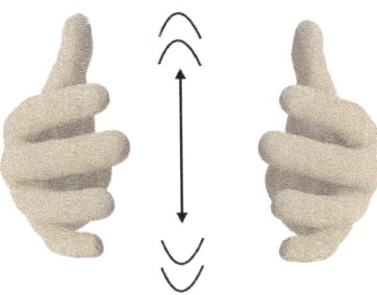

Hand gesture for sculpting

Invitation to play or showcase

Hand position for an attention call

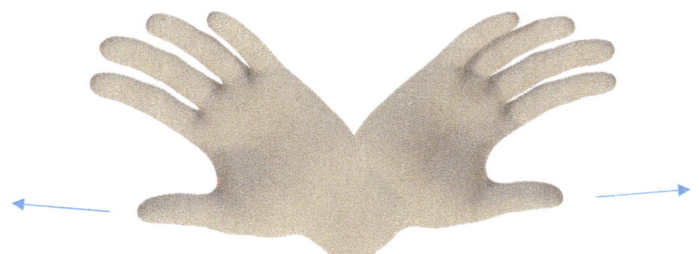

Prepare for a stop cut

stop cut the rest of the circle and have just the desired subgroup remain playing. This is useful to showcase a subgroup that has spontaneously come up with nicely interleaved parts.

One purpose of sculpting is to help the group hear all the parts that are playing within the overall mix of instruments. When you showcase a subgroup and then bring the whole group back to play along, the group can focus on aspects of the sound they might not have noticed until showcasing made those aspects apparent. Once they hear their own structures and patterns highlighted by sculpting, they can use them in their interactions in a self-directed way. With positive recognition, being highlighted can also boost the confidence of players.

Adding voices and instruments

I like to start with drumming because it is easy to get people involved playfully, and it is a great arena in which to teach facilitation interventions that will apply to all kinds of music - vocal, instrumental, and percussive. It fulfills both musicianship and leadership goals. I also start with drumming because the common rhythms and the process of entrainment is automatically bonding.

To bring voices into the drumming, I might ask the group to vocalize or "sing what you play." I am not looking for perfect mirroring; it is enough for the players to make any vocal sound that imitates their drumming. Connecting the voice and the body when making music is a skill we will approach from a number of angles, since it is central to developing fluency when manifesting musical ideas.

Another way to introduce voices is to add a layer of sound over the drumming using vocal call-and-response. I will prepare the group by making my first call informational - "I call, you answer" or "You hear me and you repeat." Then I give a simple melodic call that fills the space of 4 beats. Fancy syncopation can wait. At first it is important to make the calls easy to follow and to ensure success. Students are more self-conscious about errors as soon as we introduce melody, and this is certainly true when using voices. It helps to call the students' responses "imitation" rather than echoing or copying. This gives them permission to copy as best they can, emphasizing the effort to imitate rather than judging whether the copying was perfect.

Passing out parts and looping

The call and response melodies that I use can also be looped - that is, continuously repeated as an ostinato. Once I introduce a "keep going" or "repeat this" gesture, I can move from single calls to establishing repeating looped parts. I sculpt the group into sections and assign a different loop to each section. I sing the part with the students in each group until I am sure they can sustain it independently. Leaving them alone too soon invites rhythmic or

The Concept of the Rest of the Circle (ROC)

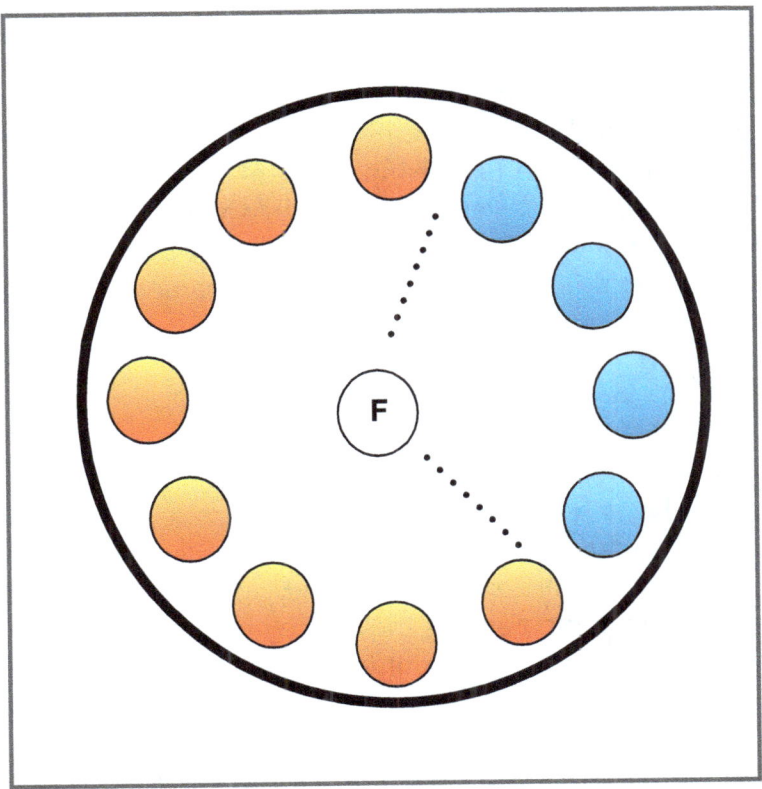

The "rest of the circle" (in orange) lies outside the facilitator's field of vision. They cannot see the facilitator's gestures. facial expressions, and body language unless the facilitator moves and faces them.

melodic chaos. This is also where I assess their capacity for complexity. If a part turns out to be too hard, that is good information for me to know, and I can quickly modify the part to be more accessible. These melodies are not generally pre-decided; I make them up each time and enjoy the opportunity to model improvisation.

If all goes well, I can have the group drumming a common rhythm and singing four different interleaved vocal parts that I modeled via call and response, then morphed into continuing loops and assigned to various sections of the group. In this activity, I am providing an example of improvisation, since I honestly do not decide on the vocal parts in advance. Modeling improvising in this way can inspire volunteers who might have a new part to offer. I can keep the rhythm going, end the vocalizing, and ask "who has a new vocal part?" If someone offers one, I can model how to turn that into a call and then into a loop. I am coaching the musicianship and the leadership elements of this activity at the same time. The volunteer might come up with several complementary parts, or classmates might. Then we have a spontaneous improvised composition of loops-over-rhythm, sometimes with soloists. This is not an unusual outcome for the opening segment of the first class.

"Make it your own"

The danger of passing out parts and having the group echo and loop the patterns is that the individual creative impulse is being temporarily put on hold. It is a noble support role to provide a solid pattern for your playing peers, but this role needs to be balanced with the creative role through which players express their individuality and identity. It is useful to turn the group loose to change the patterns they have been given. The best learning comes from playful experimenting, which in turn comes from permission to "make it your own."

Structured small ensembles - using loops for song-form group improvisation

Imagine the beginning of the Motown song "My Girl." It begins with a bass line, then a guitar riff enters, and while these parts are looping/repeating, a melody comes in to add a new layer and launch the song. In drum circle language, the parts are "layered in." This three-part model, consisting of a bass line, followed by a repeating and contrasting groove, and then a melody, will always yield a workable structure when the parts are sung and improvised. You can add in extra players by harmonizing the bass line or the riff, and you can add more soloists to encourage melodic conversations among the singers. This is a common activity at the vocal workshops run by Rhiannon, who is one of the amazing improvising singers who performs and teaches with Bobby McFerrin. The form can be summarized as: start Groove 1, add Groove 2, harmonize either groove, and lastly add a melodic solo. Rhiannon's book, *Vocal River*, contains many similar exercises for improvising vocal ensembles.

This layered vocal loop activity works well with small ensembles. It can be introduced early in a class or a workshop. Most player-singers are able to come up with a useable first loop. If needed, their part can be coached into a more friendly form or doubled with a strong singer as a partner. The next person to enter can create a complimentary part that ideally will fill some of the holes in the rhythm left by the first part. If not, I would model such a part as a suggestion. Here too, if the singer is secure enough to hold their part alone, great. If not, the part can be reinforced by a second singer. The third part, the one involving harmony, requires a person adept at harmonizing and shadowing; that is, following one of the first two parts, note for note, in harmony. When I am lucky enough to have a good harmonizer in the class, I am grateful. When a singer falters with the harmony, there are options. One is to have the singer simply double an existing part in unison. Another is to have the singer sing long tones without having to follow a melody note for note. A third is to model a harmony part and see if the singer can join it. Lastly, the fourth person who enters has freedom to melodically solo over the three existing parts.

When One Note is Enough

When we begin with rhythm, we can have access to universal aspects of our musicality. We are all moved by music, and we can translate the ways we move into sounds with our feet and hands. Players who are used to exclusively reading music are relieved to be able to drum freely before taking the risks to make notes on an instrument that could be wrong and trigger a cringe response. Sometimes I transition the class from drumming on hand drums and percussion to vocalizing their rhythms. Then I have them find their main instruments and transfer their vocal rhythm to just one note on the instrument. Now we have a rhythm jam going on instruments, but they are using their instruments mainly as drums. Next I can ask them to explore the percussion possibilities of their instruments. Besides plucking a guitar note or blowing on a flute, what other sounds can a guitar or flute make? Players will discover that a guitar can be turned over and played literally as a drum, or the pick can rub on the ribbed surface of the strings like a guiro or scratcher. Flautists will find that they can tap on the finger holes to make sounds reminiscent of a marimba. All instruments have sound possibilities that allow them to be played as simple percussion. This is a very gentle introduction to using instruments for their rhythm sounds alone. This is often a useful skill, especially whenever the music is too complex to join using notes.

For any student who experiences difficulty jumping into a group improvisation using rhythm, I will start by helping the student tap the ongoing pulse of the music. Joining the pulse is a fine first step. Next, I will coach making accents in the pulse, starting with the "one," wherever it happens to fall. Another simple exercise is to exaggerate the weaker beats to the point of silence, leaving only an accented beat or two. At this point, the student is playing a rhythm and has the pulse in their body. That's usually enough to launch their exploring.

Melodies and rhythms on instruments - Movement and Stillness, Movement and Stasis

The first segment of the class was introducing rhythm play through drum circle activities. From a musicianship perspective, this gave students the opportunity to explore their own personal creative pallet of percussion sounds, and it gave them a chance to experience their identity as a cooperative music-making group facing the unknown territory of improvisation together. The second segment introduced vocal melodic elements along with rhythm through the medium of call and response modeling and passing out interleaved rhythmic melodic parts. The activity was introduced in a large group format first, then broken down into a small ensemble format for the exploration of loop-based song form. In this format there were specific contrasting roles - creating baseline melodies, filling holes in the rhythm, harmonizing a melody, and free soloing.

Students come to class with an array of traditional and non-traditional instruments. I have seen tap shoes (as percussion), harpsichord, otamatone, and all kinds of strings and winds. To introduce instrumental improvisation on whatever instrument combinations the group has to offer, the next activity I introduce is a simplified version of the vocal layered loop quartet. In place of four contrasting roles, we move to instrumental duets in which there are just two roles - stillness and movement or stillness and stasis. Stillness is reflected in an unchanging note, or drone. As an alternative, stillness can be presented as stasis in the form of an unchanging rhythmic melody or loop. Movement is melodic exploration, in contrast to the steady drone or looped ostinato. The melodies in this duet activity thus always have a harmonic context.

I always mention the contrasts I am introducing. Contrasts - between silence and sound, between home note and any excursion away from home, between verse and chorus, between group and soloist, between dynamic levels or timbres, between stillness/stasis and movement - are the basis for generating a good deal of musical interest. Put this way, improvisation only needs to focus on creating contrasts. Each sound, like each person, has its own unique identity.

Contrasts in musical energy

Let's explore the idea that musical interest comes from contrast. A chord may be beautiful, but it becomes ordinary if it is repeated and unchanged. Change a note within a chord and the energy has changed from major to minor, or from seventh to diminished. These small contrasts create vastly different moods.

We all know musical cadences that seem to build tension and call for resolution. Withhold the last note of a familiar phrase and see how hungry the listeners are for the phrase to be completed. We enjoy musical tension and release. Every musical energy invites its opposite. After intensity we welcome calm. After peacefulness we crave action.

One way of describing outwardly exuberant energy is to call it Yea! energy This is the energy of cheers and exclamations, of calls from across a busy street, and the laser-like pointedness of the Bulgarian Women's Choir. The complementary energy of rhapsody and lullaby can be called Ooh energy. A piece that sandwiches Yea! and Ooh energies in A-B-A format will have contrasts that listeners will appreciate.

Preparing to improvise with instruments - introducing solo and support roles

I can use the duet form to isolate two contrasting roles to play in improvisation - solo and support. I will likely model this before trying to explain it in words. I ask for a volunteer who either sings or plays a single line melody instrument. I will sing or play a short melody and end on a held note, or drone. By gesture, I will invite my partner to do what I did, playing a new melody over my drone note, and ending on their own drone note. I might say, "play something that goes with this" or "explore a short melody and end with a held note." Bowed strings can hold notes forever. So can wind instruments, but the players have to breathe to renew their note. Plucked and mallet instruments need to trill to hold a note, but all instruments can do it. This game of solo-drone can go back and forth a few times, with each player experiencing the support role holding a drone and the soloist role making excursions and journeys. The key to being a sensitive supporter is to not merely hold a drone as an automaton, but to breathe and feel the soloist's expression along with them. This leads to active support that includes subtle changes in dynamics and timing – musical empathy.

Solo and Ostinato - grooves and rhythms as support

Another duet activity highlighting the solo and support roles involves the interplay of a soloist whose partner provides a repeating phrase as a platform. These roles are exchanged as the piece develops. To arrive at the repeating phrase, the first player improvises and explores melodically, settling in on a short, repeated pattern of notes. This signals the second player to begin improvising and exploring, ending with their own repeated pattern. This exchange goes back and forth a few times and can evolve into a free improvisation before finding an ending place.

Activity	Description	Support role	Solo role
Solo/drone	Play a short melody, then hold the last note as a steady drone	"homer"	"roamer"
Solo/ostinato	Play a short melody, then repeat the last phrase as a loop	"homer"	"roamer"

In improvised duets, the solo and support roles can be exchanged multiple times. One "stays home" and provides structure, the other "roams" and explores melody and rhythm before returning "home."

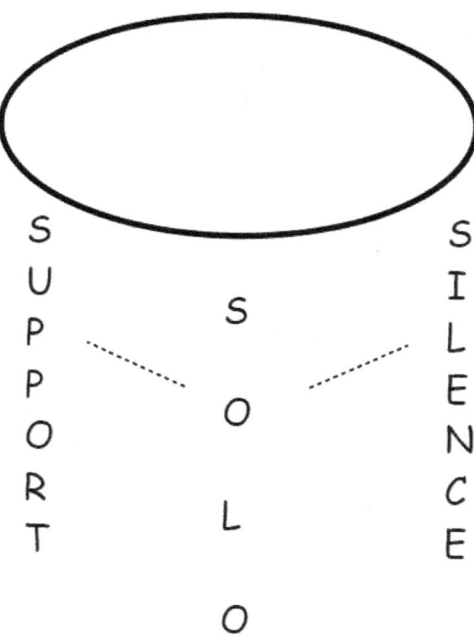

*The three-legged stool: Cohesive Social Improvisation
rests on the three pillars of solo, support and silence.
Balance these roles and all players benefit.*

Open-ended Social Music Improvisation in Quartets

Social Music Improvisation rests on a three-legged stool of solo, support, and silence. To create an improvisation from silence, members of the group first start something (anything). Once started, other members jump in and contribute contrast and support. With an improvisation ongoing, players interact and converse, and at times surrender the central focus to allow for a solo statement. The soloist will be flexible and morph back to a support role when his or her story has been told. The group members can contribute additional layers of contrast by judiciously using silence, dropping out, and returning to make the size of the group one of the elements of the music.

What have we learned so far?

We have described the basic concepts of improvisation and facilitation that will be expanded over the course of the semester. We begin with the idea of music as play. We support risk taking with everyone playing rhythms together, making the first explorations anonymous. We provide strong models of improvisation to imitate and copy via call and response activities. We explicitly give permission to take ideas and morph them creatively to "make them your own." We introduce complexity and contrast by dividing the group into sections with interleaved rhythms. We sculpt the group to isolate and highlight available contrasts in sound. We give ample free time to explore contrasts as a group. We add melody through vocal call and response. Melody and rhythm combine to create song forms. We introduce harmony through shadowing an existing part. We explore solo and support roles using drones and looped ostinato patterns.

For facilitation, we begin by introducing the basic drum circle gestures – an attention call, counting in, counting out, the stop cut, volume up and down, and sculpting. We show how to identify who is highlighted and who is in the rest of the circle, how to change dynamics and tempo via gesture, and how to solicit volunteers by invitation, rather than command. In all these activities, we let the music be the teacher by getting out of the way so the students can learn by listening to themselves and adjusting. These concepts are "what" gets taught. In the subsequent sections we will begin to explore "how" these concepts are presented in flowing sequence to deepen engagement and enhance learning, and "why" they have social and emotional impact.

Silence

Music arises from silence and returns to silence. In point of fact, we call the ambient sounds around us "silence" when we have not named any sounds that we are focusing on. Silence is a resting place in our attention, the absence of a sound object. When a piece is over, silence has claimed its place as the soloist. It takes maturity to allow and endure silences rather than fill them with chatter or idle sound-making. I always mention to students the importance of respecting silences. This helps cultivate an atmosphere of deeper and more contemplative listening. A brief moment of silence often signals the natural ending of an improvisation. Consensus is a powerful musical event when players recognize an end point.

Welcoming chaos

Chaos is an interesting and dynamic event in music that takes us beyond what is comfortable and familiar, and into new possibilities. It can be hard to listen to, as when a jam session or improvised piece deteriorates into a true "train wreck" and the music grinds to an awkward halt. Even then, there is a compositional contrast between chaos and silence. We don't often cultivate chaos in music. Shared rhythms and shared tonalities are examples of consensus and order. But there is a place for chaos. Ask a group of drummers to all do a roll simultaneously – this "rumble" is high energy, joyful or suspenseful chaos, waiting for the resolution that comes when they all stop together, which can be a potentially powerful moment. Ask a group of singers to all start singing simultaneously with strong voices, each on a note of their own choosing, unchanging, with no prepared key or coordination. The result will be a "soup" of tone cluster, with notes rubbing against each other in a variety of ways. Chaotic, but potentially interesting. Conduct a vocal group to repeatedly make this kind of "sound splash," and the sound clusters will shift from one iteration to the next, often inching towards more consensus and order.

Early in the class semester I will introduce chaos and the challenge of finding order as a group activity. Some choral directors will ask their groups to start on random notes and then task them with coming to unison without telling them how. You will see who among the group is open to change and flexibility, who will easily lend their voice to the group mind, and who will set themselves up as the model to be followed. A bit of a personality test.

Deeper support - introducing the shadow

When you are playing a sport like basketball or soccer, and you are on defense, you are tuned in to the person you are guarding, monitoring their every move while preserving your ability to react quickly if a move turns out to be a feint. If you listen to a musical playing partner in that way, you are not trying to defeat them, just to match them, no matter where they go, and keep up in real time. Call and response activities require concentration and memory to repeat melodies and rhythms. Shadowing is a more immediate skill - to as closely as possible mirror what a partner is playing, in real time. You are not so much repeating what you hear as merging listening and sound-making with minimal processing time. You are lending yourself to the musical gestures of your partner. Shadowing can be tremendously valuable in having sections sound like one instrument with one articulation and phrasing. Shadowing is like being fluent in the musical language of your partner. To build this skill, it is useful to start simply.

I teach shadowing starting with motion. I ask for a volunteer and say: "move how I move," as if we were each other's mirror image. I make sure to begin with simple, easy to track movements of an arm or my torso. I will build up to movements that involve bending or stepping, always trying to make the movements somewhat predictable. I am not trying to fool my partner, but to bring them along with me. Then I will reverse roles and say, "you start, I'll follow." After doing this movement activity in pairs, I will pick people with similar vocal ranges and have them do it vocally, without body movement. We try this with eye contact and without (the latter is harder).

We learn shadowing to prepare to support players in an improvisation when their part catches our interest, but the part may be soft in the overall mix. Doubling the part via shadowing brings the phrase to the forefront. We shadow to say "I hear you, and I like what you are playing. I'll help make it louder so others can hear it too."

Harmonizing

Of all the musical skills I have taught, harmonizing is the least simple to teach. I have seen great musicians struggle with harmony, and some musicians harmonize in sophisticated ways without being able to explain how they do it. If you experiment playing over a drone, you will experience harmony and harmonic intervals. If I give students a loop of a melody to play around with, among the things they can do is to harmonize the repeating melody. It is easier in some ways to harmonize than to improvise a fresh complementary melody from scratch, since the rising and falling melodic movements of the model melody and its rhythms are set. Another way of sneaking in harmonic experiences is to teach rounds. While the singers are focused on their own melody, the other parts of the round provide harmonic context.

Safety and Wrong Notes – There is Dignity in Risk

We emphasize making musical experiences playful to minimize self-consciousness and the inhibition that can come from being afraid to play a wrong note. It is useful to say, "there are no wrong notes" and treat all musical intervals as energies and tensions that are in flux and moving at times towards resolutions. But we have been acculturated to hear certain notes as "clinkers," cringe-worthy and potentially embarrassing if they were not intended. I try to communicate a respect for exploration and an expectation that clinkers are a welcome part of the process. Intentionally working with "wrong notes" is an exercise in growing bigger ears. It will take time for listening to expand to the point that all notes are welcome and workable. Repeating a clinker gives it context and makes it just another tension rather than an error. And what if we do make errors? It has to be permissible and part of the way we learn if we strive to live up to our motto: "there is dignity in risk." When we enter the temple of music it is a no-snark zone. Safety is enhanced by modeling supportive ways of giving feedback and by promptly correcting and reframing comments that are critical or mocking. We do not expect beginners to start as experts. We learn by doing, and we need to feel safe to try making music at our honest and authentic current ability level to hope to improve over time. If we establish ground rules that promote safe exploring in class, the biggest critic we have to face is often the inner one. The path to musical, personal, and social growth then becomes: take risks, make errors, and tame the inner critic.

Making Productive Errors

When improvising, repeating a clinker is one way to normalize it. The note becomes just another element to work with. Another technique that transforms errors comes from using the chromatic scale. We are rarely more than a half-step away from a note that will suit the harmonic context of whatever we are playing. Learning to play chromatically gives us the flexibility to shift quickly. So does sirening or sliding if your instrument permits it.

Learning by Doing

When I devote class sessions to quartet improvisation and allow the players freedom to explore and uncover their own working strategies and frustration points, they naturally uncover some of the principles that make small group improvisations work in a coordinated and satisfying way. These principles include:

> be bold, offer something for your partners to work with
> be consistent, make your playing easy for others to follow and join
> be unselfish, hear what the piece sounds like without you now and then
> be connected, play with what your partners give you.

They may also uncover more specific roles that work:

> be the drummer, provide a steady pulse or rhythm
> be the bass, offer a repeated bass line
> set the mood, play something that strongly suggests a mood or style
> leave space, play conversationally with room for others to respond.

The process of learning by doing will also likely raise questions about how the improvisations might have been more satisfying. Players may realize after the fact that they played too much or too little, that they missed opportunities to jump in or respond, or that there were options open and paths not taken that they would like to try in future improvisation sessions. It is useful to give groups a "second movement" to explore some of these paths that they did not put into action the first time.

Brave Space Contrasted with Safe Space

The goal of facilitating experiences in music improvisation is to encourage people. Encourage. To help them be brave enough to learn by doing. This involves some risk since there is no learning possible without taking the chance to try something new. The overall atmosphere must walk the line between too much safety and not enough safety. Too much safety, and the learners stay so close to their current base of knowledge and experience that they do not expand. Too little safety, and the learners may not take any risks at all. So how can leaders create and sustain "Brave Space?"

In the original quote by Lao Tsu that inspired the title "Return to Child" for Music for People's book about David Darling's teaching, the phrase concludes – "the child within us is Simple and Daring enough to live the Secret (of Nature)." Simple and Daring. The way to encourage people to be daring is to keep the activities disarmingly simple. You are not "improvising," you are "noodling," "telling a story," or being playful. Play is simple and self-rewarding. Simplicity can create depth. Play a solo, just on one note. It becomes a rhythm game, while eliminating potential angst about wrong notes.

Celebrate risk taking. Be enthusiastic when people step in and volunteer, and when they reach for new levels of engagement in their sounds.

Trust that experience will teach. Music making is more physical than cerebral.

Simple and Daring.

There is Dignity in Risk.

Thus far, we have introduced thirteen improvisation skills:

1. Sing what you play, Play what you sing
2. Ooh energy - rhapsody and lullaby
3. Yea! energy - strong calls for celebration or warning
4. Musical conversations with group partners
5. Shadowing - imitation in real time
6. Harmonize what a partner is playing
7. Match pulse and create accents
8. Ostinato - play a consistent groove
9. Use your instrument as a drum
10. Drone - play one unchanging note
11. Chromatic - explore using half steps
12. Do as much as you can with only one note
13. Play as many "wrong notes" as possible

These skills have been the central content of the Music for People workshops originated by the late cellist David Darling and are described in the book written about his teaching, *Return to Child*. Coincidentally, they also comprise the thirteen cards that are categorized as Basic Skills in an improvisation teaching tool, the *Music Doctor Improv Card* set (see Appendix).

In the midst of an all-improvised event, a solo singer has the support of a quartet and a room full of hands.

For beginning improvisers, I present four roles to choose among. We teach and practice each role before combining them:

Start Something

Jump In/Join In

Support What You Hear

Stand Out/Solo

(From the www.MusicConstructEd.com website, part of a lesson plan called "In The Groove," covering the scaffolding and sequencing of skills for group improvisation.)

Support, solo, or be attentively silent - find the moment to contribute your sound.

Part Two - Going Beyond the Basics

Using Contrast and Silence

This set of activities emphasizes ways of creating contrast and contributing to an improvisation by using silence judiciously. These skills require social as well as musical awareness to decide when would be the best time to drop out or enter an improvisation, and how one can contribute sounds with emotional impact to express individuality, or actively create drama and conflict for an artistic effect.

Silence as a Contribution to an Ensemble

There is no greater and simpler contribution to an improvisation than to wait to enter or to temporarily drop out after playing a while. In small ensemble improvisations, group size is an important compositional element. A quartet sounds different from a trio, duet, or soloist. A soloist sounds different in an a cappella context as contrasted with a solo accompanied by others playing instruments. When I teach the value of silence, I am mindful to make the suggestion gently, so it is not taken as "please don't play." The best wording I have found is "listen to what the piece sounds like without you now and then." I want the players to feel free to enter and leave, because they contribute contrast with either action.

Contrasts of emotional energy

One way of inviting people to solo is to call it a solo. That will intimidate some players, even experienced ones. But they can be encouraged to play expressively if the solo is called by another name, such as "tell us a story" in the music. I am aiming for creating a safe place to explore so that eventually players can risk unleashing the full emotional range and power of their expression, no matter what the emotional content might be. We welcome joy and sadness, pain and prayer, frustration and fulfillment. But playing with authentic emotion is not just emoting - the coordination and the timing of the person's statement will impact whether the message comes through with social support and the other players grasp and support the story.

Coyotes

We sometimes have players who "do not play well with others." Or the energy of the emotion being expressed is pointedly obnoxious or antisocial. One game we play in class in preparation for such situations is to assign one player to be a disruptor or trickster/coyote. For example, if the group is playing percussion and drums together, one player is assigned to do all he or she can to influence the group to lose the pulse, get fuzzy with the rhythm, or abandon the groove. This prepares the group to listen deeply enough to resist disorganizing influences. In practice, it does not matter if the person who "marches to a different drummer" intends to disrupt or is innocently independent, the listening task for the rest of the group remains "stay together no matter what."

Polyrhythms – multiple ways to organize the rhythm

Part of musicianship is being able to stick to your own part, strongly, no matter what the contrasting or competing parts might be. This is necessary for there to be polyrhythmic music with more than one way of parsing the meter, as when a phrase in 4/4 time is played simultaneously with a phrase in 3/4 time. One way of adding contrast to an improvisation is to introduce new rhythms. We introduce this with games that start with everyone playing a common pulse. The group is then divided so that one section accents every 4th beat, another every third beat, and another every 6th or 8th beat. Still more variety can be introduced with other odd meters, such as every 5th or 7th beat. Perceptually, these layered polyrhythmic patterns can take a while to come into clear listening focus. It helps to stay with these patterns long enough for the listeners to become slightly entranced by the repetition. The metric centers can shift - the overall patterns that emerge from the combination of mixed meters can be like the visual figure/ground examples that sometimes are seen as two faces and sometimes as two goblets. We organize the perceptual information in a variety of ways, all of which are legitimate. As a player in an ongoing improvisation, a simple skill to master is to find the overall pulse. By adding accents in the pulse every 3rd, 4th, or 5th beat, a player can introduce polyrhythmic complexity in an accessible way. The next step might be to turn the simple pulse into a repeated melodic phrase. If a group of players improvise in this style, their music will resemble the minimalist composers.

New ways of approaching an instrument

I accept it as a given that all sounds can have musical uses. There are traditional techniques for every instrument - ways of playing violin or oboe that will allow players to read written music and participate in organized bands and orchestras. But the sound that might be most apropos in a certain situation might not be one that is reachable with standard technique. It might involve removing the mouthpiece and blowing through the woodwind as a tube; it might involve playing that area of a string instrument between the bridge and the tailpiece. It might involve using the instrument to imitate a human exclamation, or an animal sound, or a sound of nature. Improvisation requires the courage and explorer spirit to "boldy go" even if no one has gone there before. This might mean bowing a music stand to bring out the resonant frequency or using articles of clothing (flip-flops) as mallets. When the operating principle is that "there are no wrong notes," we may find, in the words of Rumi, that "we have fallen into the place where everything is music."

Exploring Support Roles

The next set of improvisation skills emphasizes ways of being of support to your playing partners. They include concrete skills such as offering a bass pattern and more abstract social interactions, such as playing in ways that influence the direction of the group through imitation and inspiration.

Support Via Flexibility

In preparing students to improvise in small ensembles, a lot of attention is given to ways of supporting the contributions of one's playing partners. Certain instrumental roles emphasize support, as is the case for the traditional "rhythm section" of bass and drums. However, one can fulfill the role of the bass player or the drummer on any instrument. When you hear that the music would benefit from the organizing structure and predictability of a bass line or a groove, players can use their instrument to make those contributions with a bass line played on flute, or a percussive scratched rhythm can come from guitar with muted strings.

Two sides of Imitation - Use What They Give You and Start a Conversation

One of the most important concepts in ensemble improvisation is imitation. When you imitate the sounds, rhythms, and melodies of a partner, you are communicating that you heard them and are interested in interacting. Imitation does not have to be a literal copy. What is critical is the intent to interact. For example, sometimes when I give a call in a call and response activity, the response I get back is different from the call. That information is always useful. If my call was too complex, or the set up for the call was unclear, or the group was too distracted to fully listen, I will get a less detailed response - "leveling," you might call it. I can use that information to make the next call shorter, simpler, and more accessible.

In an ongoing improvisation, a player may want to exactly copy a musical statement that originates with one of their partners but may not be able to catch all of the notes on the fly. In these cases, imitation is a thoroughly legitimate way of interacting. You might only be able to match the home note, or only be able to match the rhythm without any of the notes. If you want to encourage interactions, it helps to practice this kind of impressionistic imitation that is not literal. Celebrate the attempts and emphasize what the students did correctly. More sophisticated imitation will come with practice and experience.

For those students with perfect pitch or well-developed relative pitch on their instrument, they may have no trouble locating home notes and the tonal centers of their partners. For everyone else, practice playing with chromatic scales can help them learn to quickly locate tonal centers and mask their searching.

When you incorporate improvisation into teaching, you do not have to have every activity preplanned and programmed in advance. Just as an improviser is ready to interact with the other players in an ensemble, as a teacher I can see what the group is giving me in their unplanned improvising that I can capitalize on and use for a teaching purpose. If something spontaneously happens in the group that matches a concept I would like to expand on, I can step into the facilitator role and showcase those players.

For example, if I intend to teach harmonizing and shadowing a vocal part, as many backup singers do, I may look to see if any of the group members spontaneously create a duet singing in harmony within a larger group improvisation. If so, I might fade down the rest of the group to showcase the harmonizers, and then invite the other players to join the harmony so they can experience it for themselves. I might fade down each harmony part separately to highlight how each one sounds in isolation, then give the group the signal to resume improvising on their own.

Fugue and imitation

I worked with cellist David Darling for many years in his organization, Music for People. He originated many improvisation activities that were simplifications and variations on traditional music styles. I use his game of fugue to practice imitation with my students. The game resembles "telephone," but in this game it is a musical phrase that is passed around the circle. The goal is to repeat the phrase accurately, but part of the humor of the game is the way the phrase morphs as it is passed from person to person. When the phrase is passed in a steady rhythm, the resulting music sounds like a fugue's multiple staggered entrances. I often introduce the game using Baroque-era melodies, real or imitated. The first player puts out a strong short melody, and then does the equivalent of murmuring - playing notes that fill the space and stay in rhythm, but which are not meant to be memorable or copied. The second player repeats (or imitates) the first strong phrase, then murmurs to fill the space. This repeats around the group until every player has entered and murmured. When the phrase comes back around to the first player, he or she starts a new phrase that is copied and passed around the circle. Besides the focus on imitation, the game also gives the players the opportunity to fill the space with total improvisational freedom, as they can murmur in any way they wish, all the while staying responsive and supporting the overall key, tempo, and style of the piece. Depending on the available time, the next phase of the game may involve any player, at any time, offering a new strong phrase for imitation.

Sophisticated tonal support - Chords and harmony

Many of the techniques that foster improvisational opportunities involve serving in a support role. For example, when I play repeated chord progressions at the piano or on guitar, it invites students to experiment, improvising melodic lines over the repeated chords. At first, the safest path for new improvisers to take is to play long tones over the chords. They can experience the ways the held notes create tension and release as the chord accompaniment affects the harmonic meaning of the long tones. Then they can move on to longer phrases and craft their own melodies. In the second half of the class, when the emphasis is equally on leadership and musicianship, each student will get the opportunity to lead a group improvisation starting with chord progressions of their choosing.

Descending scales

There are too many workable chord progressions to name, but there are a few that are good starting places. Play a descending scale in waltz time from c down to g in the left hand on piano, changing notes on the downbeat of each new measure. In the right hand, on the second and third beats of each measure, play a c chord until the last beat, then change to a g chord. This is the core of the song "Bo Jangles." Play a descending minor scale in 4/4 time with similar minor chords and the song is "Hit the Road, Jack." The experience involves the tension and release of the V chord returning to the I chord. Other basic chord progressions that are simple and invite improvised melodies include the "Heart and Soul" progression from I to VI min to II min to V, and what is often called "the four-chord song," I - V - VI min - IV.

Social support

There are simple ways to support a partner in an improvisation. You can be silent and leave them space to shine, you can find their pulse or their rhythm and serve as their attentive drummer, you can identify their melodic or harmonic context and support them with chords or conversational melody lines, etc. But how do you go about asking for attention within the context of an improvisation, without using words, just using the music itself? This is an exercise in strategic playfulness. You could ask for attention by creating contrasts - you could play extremely softly and use matching dramatic body language, or you could play at cross-purposes with your partners, or be extremely loud and insistent - any of these may serve the purpose. Similarly, you can be the connector in an improvisation by finding a common pulse or common harmony tones. In a group with players from very disparate styles (classical and folk music, for example) I sometimes match the style of one partner and slowly morph my playing to see if I can bring them along to join the style of another group member.

Drones and ostinatos

When I set up musical opportunities to improvise, I start by keeping things simple. If offer support in the form of a steady unchanging drone note, beginning improvisers have a predictable home base to return to. In addition, every note they play with a drone accompaniment is an interval, so while the student is playing a simple melody, automatically there is a harmonic context provided by the drone that adds interest and complexity. Later on I can verbally identify "playing a drone note for a partner" as one of the key support roles a person can serve in an improvising ensemble.

The rhythmic counterpart to a drone is a short, repeated phrase. Depending on your musical reference point, that would be called an ostinato, a groove, a hook, or a bass line. Such short, repeated phrases provide a predictable tonal center and a reliable rhythm and pace. Similar to a drone, holding an ostinato pattern for a partner is a valuable support role.

Using Current, Historical, and Personal Musical Styles

These improvisation skills emphasize the ways we can include our favorite types of music in our playing, expressing who we are through our musical languages and dialects, telling stories in sound with and without words.

Every student comes from a home base of musical experience, with a history of immersion in a variety of musical styles. The tonalities and instrument combinations that are most familiar to us come from our ancestry – what our parents danced to in the house, what our worship music consisted of, whether our childhood songs came from Sesame Street or grandmother's record collection, and eventually, what music we chose for ourselves in our early and later teen years. This process of acculturation shapes each person's musical imagination when we improvise as soloists. We want to welcome every influence. In the accompanist and support roles, we need to be open to learning about the musical home bases of our playing partners, so we can meet them where they are and complement their sounds. It helps to be conversant in the language of blues, funk, pop, salsa, country, metal, and a variety of classical music styles. Your ears will be even larger if you include the tonalities of far-flung cultures.

There is a longstanding tradition in jazz improvisation to sneak snippets of known melodies into improvised solos. These bits and pieces can be spontaneous, as when a player has a "that reminds me of a tune" moment, and they are fluent enough to use their own association process to fuel their improvisation. Sometimes there is an intent to pay tribute to another musician using their well-known melodies, woven into the fabric of an improvised solo. These are creative ways of putting our home base of music into action.

When we access and harness our emotions, we can deeply express our authentic self in sound. This honesty and vulnerability can make for very open and intimate music that impacts both the players and the listeners, although some players fear that emotionality can't be played with control, and they hesitate to take that risk. But "making it real" is a pathway to powerful music and powerful social interactions, playing from the heart.

Sometimes, improvised music will inspire spontaneous lyrics that can help make the emotional messages of the music more transparent. And in the other direction, improvised spoken words and lyrics can inspire the players to create the right mood as an accompaniment.

Some of the techniques we include as aspects of Social Music Improvisation are meant to subtly effect our playing partners. We play in ways that make us "influencers," connecting and inspiring our playing partners to join our energy and style, be it loud dance music that generates infectious rhythm, or a whisper-soft mood for suspense, reflection, or peacefulness.

As a contemplative exercise, when we suggest that people play something familiar extra slowly, we are asking them to re-introduce themselves to the piece, note by note and interval by interval. There will be nuances discovered at this slower pace that would have been overlooked. It is easy to get caught up in the physical effort of producing the notes and tempting to run through the routine of getting from the beginning to the end of a familiar piece of music. And what gets sacrificed is the listening, which was and is the most important element. Playing extra slowly lets the player, and all of the partners who are playing along, listen differently and more deeply than usual.

The collection of Social Music Improvisation skills would not be complete without mentioning how important it is to maintain a playful attitude. When the moment calls for levity, let yourself be the clown in the group. Life and art can be serious pursuits, but we are renewed every time we let our sense of humor lighten the mood, make the most of everyone's errors, and welcome the unexpected.

Making music is natural when children grow up in a nurturing musical environment.

Part Three - Social Music Improvisation and Social Emotional Learning

Social Emotional Learning (SEL) advocates want to help people to be more self-aware, more adept at controlling strong emotions, and more kind, sensitive, and appropriately assertive in their social interactions. But it is difficult to construct experiences that require these skills in a contained way suitable for classrooms, even though that would be the most impactful approach. Learning SEL concepts through role-play and literary examples are at least one step removed from direct experience. Embedding SEL lessons into everyday classroom experiences is ideal, but doing so requires staff to master counseling content in addition to their subject area curricula.

One form of social interaction that is presentable in classroom settings is group music improvisation. Many key components of SEL are well represented in the non-verbal interactions that take place during small group music improvisation as practiced in Music for People and Rhythmic Connection workshops. This approach is documented in the books, *Return to Child* (by James Oshinsky) and *Innovative Drum Circles* (by Mary Knysh). It is also featured in the CD *The Darling Conversations* (with David Darling and Julie Weber). What distinguishes these methods from other musical offerings is their inclusion of spontaneous interpersonal music interactions using forms of free improvisation. For the sake of clarity, we will use the term Social Music Improvisation to indicate musical teaching that includes or leads to open ended social interaction in music with minimal constraints. It is the lack of constraints that requires participants to practice social self-regulation.

These activities are the musical analog of verbal conversation, in which the content is not pre-planned, the exchanges are spontaneous, and the purpose of participating is to be authentic and connected to the other musicians. By engaging in social improvisation in music, players learn a variety of musicianship skills that are also social life lessons.

Social Emotional Learning elements in music improvisation

Social Music Improvisation activities involve active listening, sensitive responding, and adjustments to social cues. They also allow for individual self-expression, often of meaningful emotions and feelings. Social Music Improvisation activities are spontaneous and unplanned, as are most verbal conversations. However, unlike exchanges in words, Social Music Improvisation activities are not dependent on language skills, so they are accessible to people with limited English experience. They provide the opportunity to learn social lessons through rewarding musical play. Participants learn the value of their own contribution to a group sound or rhythm and learn the place of honest emotion in musical self-expression. They learn the cooperation skills necessary to take turns and blend with peers. And they learn these positive social lessons most deeply when they are presented in an accepting and encouraging environment. When the music is coherent, it is because the group has cooperated and resisted distracting or negative influences. Positive social skills are an inseparable part of group music improvisation.

The Basic Activities of Social Music Improvisation

Among the first activities of any Social Music Improvisation class or event will be opportunities to entrain together in a common rhythm, attune to a common tonality, answer and echo musical statements, and express individuality through explicit permission to make your own music, original and never-before heard. There will also be collaborations in groups of two, three, or more players where the nature and direction of the music emerges from the commitment and the connections among the players.

Listening

It is inherent in improvised musical interactions that the most central skill is empathic listening. To make spontaneous music with one or more peers requires sustained focus on what the other players are contributing, and constant adjustments in one's own contributions to keep them musically compatible. These are social skills presented and enacted in a musical context. Embedding social interactions in music improvisation makes the practice self-rewarding and less prone to resistance. Spontaneous group music also calls on participants to access expressiveness. Music making is not mainly an intellectual activity; people feel the music and respond intuitively and emotionally. When their reactions are linked to their abilities to make sounds with voices or instruments, they can have socially integrated moments that reflect authentic emotional engagement, without verbal labels that require articulate vocabulary skills. Of course, people can also learn to be more adept musicians through these practices.

Entraining in rhythm

When a beat or a pulse is presented with an invitation to join in, each player is being asked to join a musical community with a consensus of where the rhythm lies and a group mind for where the rhythm will go next. The ability to join and follow a dynamically changing rhythm is a social skill. Some players will find it challenging just to detect and match the pulse or basic beat. Others will naturally blend with the rhythms they are hearing, as they are able to match their listening with their motor control for tapping rhythms on their laps or on hand drums. Still others will be trend-setters, creating new rhythms and variations that their playing partners may accept and follow, or their patterns may venture too far out and will be ignored. These interactions take place without verbal labels, which also generally means without too much ego investment in the outcome. No one is rejected and no one is exalted. The music itself, a product of group collaboration, does the teaching.

Attunement

Another arena for potential social agreement is tonality. If a group sings a unison note, there is a sense of community and commonality. If a group sings a repeated melody as a chant, there are opportunities to join the melody in its basic form and also to enhance the melody with harmonies and with complimentary melodies. These create novel and interesting rhythmic interplay. The variations will nonetheless share the common tonal center.

When a person participates in a group activity that involves entrainment or attunement, the person is having a social experience of matching their group, and thereby belonging to the group. When the group is large enough to sustain its rhythm and tonal center despite not everyone always being in unison, the group accepts variations as new energies that enhance and expand the group. Musical groups can serve as examples of inclusion, acceptance, and growth via synergy.

Collaboration

When peers gather to make music together, everyone's contribution is welcome, and no one knows exactly what the outcome will be. Some player's contributions will be melodic ideas or a certain mood. Other players will offer support by matching the pulse, adding harmony, and making space through their use of silence. Players will trade ideas and interact by repeating what they hear, imitating what they can't exactly repeat, and offering variations that reflect their individuality. These serendipitous collaborations yield artistic and unpredictable results.

Social reciprocity

The first model of social exchange at a Social Music Improvisation event might come in the form of call and response. A leader will model a rhythm or a melody for the group to emulate or echo. It is also a common event for the calls to be given by volunteers among the group. In musical form, calls demonstrate whether a person's statements are accessible to their peers or whether they are confusing. This is useful social feedback. When the calls are able to be repeated by the group, the caller experiences acceptance and belonging. When the calls are not understood by the group, the caller has the opportunity to learn from the experience and make adjustments. Either way, the group is accepting the member's attempt to connect and supporting the risk taken in making a personal statement.

At Social Music Improvisation classes and events, improvised duets spotlight the conversational roles of soloist and supporter. When a player holds an unchanging drone note for a partner, the partner has the freedom to explore and experiment in tones and rhythms. Their sounds will be heard in the social context provided by the drone, which is at the same time a harmonic context. The two descriptions refer to the same phenomenon, one from a music education point of view and the other from a social emotional learning or clinical point of view. As the player experiments with sound while a partner holds a drone, the player may be telling an expressive story, communicating emotion, and taking risks to allow themselves to be heard. Having this happen in music allows expression while masking any verbal labeling of the content. In the next phase of this activity, the roles of soloist and supporter are reversed. Both players get to experience the satisfaction of being the steadfast supporter and the bold and brave explorer. The timing of the turnover from one role to the other is not preset, as it depends on the two partners using nonverbal cues such as eye contact, breathing, and subtle body gestures to indicate when the shift might happen. Dynamic turn-taking is authentic, organic, and driven by the creative musical collaboration of the two players.

The ultimate goal in a Social Music Improvisation event is to prepare the players to join an all-improvised ensemble of four or more players. In this setting, players bring their willingness to stand out and be heard, and their ability to stand back and support the statements of others. With a combination of boldness and generosity they are able to follow the music as it emerges, staying attentive and flexible, for the sake of hearing how the art of their connectedness manifests in sound. Along the way, they also gain experience in the main content areas of Social Emotional Learning.

Traditionally, SEL covers 5 areas (CASEL, 2020):

Scott Edgar, affiliated with ArtsEdSEL.org, presents three basic principles of SEL: Identity (*Who am I and how do my prior experiences influence my decisions and mindsets?*), Belonging (*Who are we and how is our space conducive to vulnerability and trust?*), and Agency (*How do I/We make a difference?*).

The core activities of Social Music Improvisation organizations such as Music for People and Rhythmic Connections provide experience in social musical interactions that support many of these same areas of functioning - *What are my musical sources? In groups, how do I contribute and how am I changed by the experiences? How do I use music in my life?*

Mindfulness in music

If we ask: what is the highest level of social musicianship? The answer is this: The person is able to flexibly serve multiple roles in a variety of playing situations, including being an initiator, a supporter, and an attentive witness. The person is able to solo boldly and expressively when called for and inspires others with the accessibility and emotionality of their playing. The person is able to support others by adapting to the timing, tonality and musical styles of their playing partners. The person is attuned to the social relationships inherent in musical ensembles and is able to leave space for others when needed. They serve the music before they serve themselves.

In SEL terminology, the person is self-aware and able to identify and appropriately express their emotional states. The person is empathetic and able to identify and respond to the emotional states of others. The person is able to be passionate in their statements without crossing boundaries or being hurtful. The person knows their limits and self-inhibits when needed. The person is able to take pride in serving others, in balance with having their own needs met.

Social Music Improvisation is SEL without words. The activities of Music for People and Rhythmic Connections provide painless ways to experience the main areas of SEL while also developing personal and ensemble musicianship. The personal qualities that characterize a good musician also make for a self-aware and socially responsible individual.

Tuning in to a Group Improvisation

Entrainment	Attunement
Put the rhythm in your body	Sing what you play
Find the pulse	Find the home note
Match the pulse	Match the home note
Create accents in the pulse	Harmonize the home note
Just play the accents	Find a compatible melody
Play a compatible rhythm	Find compatible chords

Coordinating and synchronizing with a group starts with body involvement, moving to the beat, or singing along. From there, find the common elements of the group sound: the rhythmic pulse and the home note of the tonality. Match them, then create variations.

The Social Emotional Learning aspects of the major Return to Child activities for Social Music Improvisation

Call and Response – strong statements, clear leadership, invitations to imitate

Improvisation is not just making things up out of thin air. Creative musical play also involves taking melodies and sounds that are available as models to imitate. Sometimes the goal is to step into another person's musical shoes and reproduce what they did as closely as you can. At other times the goal is to use the model as a jumping off point for personal creativity, as we do whenever we "make something our own" by adding our own variations to what we hear.

Imitation and paraphrase are exercises in both focused attention and empathy. Can you reproduce the notes when someone plays or sings a short melody? Can you also reproduce the notes with the same energy and feeling as the original? We have all heard songs re-interpreted by different artists. The Star-Spangled Banner sounds very different played by a marching band and played as a guitar solo by Jimi Hendrix. When we make a song our own, we are using the structure of the song to express something personal and unique. Composers call it "variations on a theme." It is a longstanding tradition in music.

Call and response is a very powerful teaching tool. When a leader gives a call for a class to follow, the format of the activity is experiential education featuring imitation. The content can be anything the leader wants to showcase. A music teacher giving a lesson on major and minor can give calls in both modes, and students will experience what it sounds like and what it feels like to produce the sounds. A teacher giving a lesson on how melodies convey emotion can give calls that are happy, excited, scared, sad, irritated, bored, surprised, etc., and students will experience these emotions in musical form.

Call and response is also an opportunity for group bonding and coordination. It is no coincidence that calls and responses are part of cheers at athletic events; the calls bring together the group that sings together. We experience belonging and security when there is a strong, solid rhythmic model to follow.

Leaders can use call and echo for group bonding and they can use a call that permits variation in the answers to encourage individual self-expression.

The role of the caller in call and response is a powerful leadership position. When a person gives a call and hears their own call come back in the group's response, they experience acceptance of their contribution. When the group struggles to answer a call, the leader gets feedback about whether their statement was accessible or not. Was the call clear? Was it on the beat? Was it more complicated than the group could manage? Did the caller's body language help the group reply to the call? What simplification can the caller make to have the group respond more successfully? These are all elements of social awareness and social integration that impact not just music, but all public communication.

When we use the term "call and response" we can refer to several related, but not identical activities. Call and echo is very useful for teaching, when you want the listeners to be focused enough for the response to be identical to the call. Call and imitate allows for the response to be an attempt to reproduce the call, whether or not the responders succeed. This is useful to encourage participation without pressure from high expectations. Call and answer shows awareness of musical and verbal tropes, where the answer can complete the phrase started by the call. Finally, call and converse is what we do in most inquiries, where the response to a question is not a repetition of the question, new information follows.

Variations of Call and Response

Variation	Call	Response
Call and echo	Hey-yo	Hey-yo
Call and imitate	Taka tiki taki ta	Tata kiki taka ta
Call and answer	Shave and a haircut	Two bits
Call and converse	How's it going?	Doing great!

Every call does not require a carbon-copy response. Some calls are meant as conversation, others have expected replies that complete a phrase. Imitation of a call is sometimes the closest a player can get to the original, when they have limitations in listening or in the ability to reproduce sounds.

One Quality Sound – the good side of "me, me, me"

In the One Quality Sound activity, two or more players breathe together and agree to produce their own unique sounds all at one time. This results in an unpredictable tone cluster that is sometimes pleasing and sometimes dissonant. The challenge for each player is to stay with the note they started with, without "sweetening" or retuning their note to match their partners. This is an exercise in peer acceptance and equality. The "we" of the ensemble is made up of several strong "me's," each holding their own individual notes. All of the contributions are valued equally in this activity, and the resulting tone quality is taken in and appreciated without having to change it. Some players find it hard to avoid the social magnetism of agreement, and they are quick to modify their notes to accommodate their peers. They have difficulty "holding their own" in a group setting. Practicing One Quality Sound can help players get stronger at maintaining their sound identity and integrity in a group.

If a group values traditional harmony and precise intonation, that is important and necessary for some forms of music. But the tunings that constitute correct intonation change from historical period to historical period, and from genre to genre. Bent notes in blues, rock, and jazz have their own beauty. Equal temperament on piano makes it equally out of tune in all keys as contrasted with how string players more exactly intonate on unfretted fingerboards. The combination and difference tones that result from small gaps in tuned bells create the "shimmering" of Balinese music. In this light, One Quality Sound is an exercise in developing "big ears" to appreciate and accept the qualities of tone combinations, and thereby accept the people who are making the tones as well. It is also an exercise in standing up for oneself and maintaining one's identity in a complex social environment.

One Quality Groove – the transformation of "me, me, me" to "we"

This activity involves players starting a group sound not with a single held note, but each with a specific repeating groove of his or her own. The activity asks the players to discover one group groove that they all agree upon as quickly as possible. When the groove is discovered and all players are playing exactly the same rhythmic groove, the activity has reached its goal. The idea is to move quickly from "me" to "we," sharing individual ideas and collaborating to swiftly find a common groove. This requires players to give up any rigid attachment they may have to their own contribution for the sake of the group.

Find a Unison Pitch – me to we

As in One Quality Groove, this activity involves non-verbal group cooperation and consensus. It calls on participants to be sensitive to the group mind or community wisdom. Players start together and move to one common pitch as quickly as possible. While emphasizing flexibility, non-attachment and consensus, the activity also leaves room for each participant to contribute his or her own strong voice.

Lead with Body Language – immediate feedback

The opportunity to lead a group is eagerly desired by some students and feared and avoided by others. Unlike public speaking, conducting a group to start a sound involves only an inhale and an exhale, the first to cue and prepare the group, and the second to show them when to make their sounds. Having the group follow a leadership cue provides feedback to the leader to be socially present and accessible, tuned-in to the group, and connected via eye contact and hand gestures. When a leader is not present or unclear, the group will struggle to follow in an organized way. If the teacher focuses on self-correction and learning by reflection (e.g.- "What can you do differently to get the group to be ready to follow you?"), the student can experience increasing levels of interpersonal effectiveness as a leader.

Ooh energy and Yay! energy – emotional expressiveness

Social Emotional Learning includes being aware of feelings, expressing feelings accurately, and being able to both receive and give signals indicating common emotions. Younger children differentiate fewer emotions than older ones do, which is why they may describe themselves as feeling "bad" or "upset" without access to more descriptive words. Developing a musical vocabulary of emotions can start simply, with the sounds "ooh" and "Yay!" Ooh rhymes with "woo." It is the energy of a lullaby or a heartfelt prayer. Yay! is exuberance and excitement. This is the sound we naturally make when we cheer at an athletic event, or when we warn someone who is about to injure themselves. Musical interest often comes from simple contrasts. Using ooh energy and Yay! energy can create an interesting piece of music in A-B-A or "Oreo cookie" format. As students get older, they are able to describe more nuances of feeling, and distinguish among similar feelings such as amused, happy, elated, and over the moon.

A-B-A – contrast and journeys

Musical interest is built on contrasts. A note that is repeated becomes a perceptual reference point. Emotionally, it represents home and predictability. A change in a repeated note is immediately noteworthy. It starts a journey and can carry an emotional story. And if the original note returns, the journey ends where it began. The simplest journey is the Return to Child game of "Sah," in which a note is established, raised a small amount, and then there is a return to the starting place. A two-note story. It is also a very basic example of A-B-A form.

A-B-A can also be used with longer journeys and longer pieces of music representing home. Many popular songs have a verse and a chorus, or a repeated section followed by a bridge. When the music is improvised, the B section can be different from the A section in any number of ways, so long as the contrast is noticeable and sets up the return home. The B section can be in a different key, or use different instrumentation, or involve only a subset of the players. The B section can express a different mood or energy. When improvising in A-B-A form, the players might create consensus spontaneously. Or they might agree in advance to play "happy-sad-happy," and work out on their own when to transition and how to find agreement on the specific expressions of the contrasting emotions. A-B-A is a natural sequence for our emotional expressions. We are in a pleasant mood, then we encounter a stressor and we cry or yell. We have been pushed into a state that requires sound-making to discharge energy and restore ourselves. And when the sound-making has done its job, we are once again at a point of emotional equilibrium.

Solo-drone and Solo-ostinato: Movement and Stillness, Movement and Stasis

There is a support person. That person embodies constancy and reliability by holding a sustained drone note or repeating a short pattern of notes. To be counted on for support is an unselfish and valuable role in music and in life. The backup musician also "has your back."

There is a soloist. Given the platform of support, the soloist is free to explore self-expression boldly and creatively. Most importantly, the roles of soloist and support person are temporary and can be exchanged. No one is excluded from exploring or is locked into a routine or a rut. Each person's exploration tells their own unique story that can be acknowledged and appreciated. The support person reflects stillness – their note is unchanging and defines the tonality. The soloist reflects movement – their explorations contrast with stillness but are always perceived in the context provided by their partner. The overall music evolves in unpredictable ways, like a drawing in which two people alternate making unbroken lines. This activity bests suits instruments that can sustain notes for long periods of time, such as winds, bowed strings and voices. Plucked and struck instruments can roll or trill to sustain the drone.

The model for social interaction is a conversation. It involves turn-taking and some meaningful connection between the statements of the participants/players. Consider the structure above for interacting in music: as in a verbal conversation, the notes of one player are heard in the context of the held note from their partner's exploring. The players experience the relationship between the held note and the melody; it creates a harmonic context. The players are practicing music; but they are also demonstrating patience and active listening. They are hearing their own notes in a social setting; and by taking turns and building on each other's contributions, they are creating something unique that neither could have created alone.

For instruments that do not hold notes, and for a rhythmic extension of the solo/drone activity, the players can end their solos with a repeated rhythmic loop of their last few notes. This creates a pattern or a groove. This is very similar to the social role that bass players serve in their ensembles, holding the rhythm and the tonality with a reliable, unchanging pattern of notes. Whether the support is taking place as a drone (stillness) or as a groove (stasis), the supporting player can make their support active and sensitive, changing the volume or timing to match the energy of the soloist in the moment.

The activity requires players to serve both roles – that of the brave solo explorer and that of the solid supporter. More timid players can benefit from experience in the explorer role, and more isolated, self-absorbed or unfocused players can benefit from experience in the support role.

In the context of improvising in larger ensembles, the basic techniques of solo/drone and solo/ostinato will always be welcome contributions, although the partner relationships will be dynamic and in flux. Ending a solo with a constant tone or bass line lets the other players know when a player has finished their statement, and it opens up the solo space for other players, or for another group collaboration. The overall music evolves in unpredictable ways.

Descending Scale in Waltz Time – finding holes and opportunities to fit in

The Descending Scale in Waltz Time activity highlights two roles: solo and support. Starting on the downbeat, a player (typically a pianist or guitarist) plays a descending scale in the bass register, punctuated by chords on beats two and three. The person providing the scale and chords is "hosting the party," serving as the foundation and structure. This gives the soloist(s) the space to explore their individual creativity. Service and support are un-selfish ways of participating and can be showcased as noble and necessary. When an accompaniment is offered with reliable timing and sensitive adjustments to the mood and energy of the soloist, it elevates the power of the music. The soloist's job is to find the holes in the music that the support person provides. In the case of the Descending Waltz, the downward moving scale notes take place on the "one" of each measure, leaving holes to fill on beats two and three. The two roles form an elegant complimentary duet.

The structure of the descending scale is like walking down a flight of stairs. There is freedom to play and improvise melodies in between the steps, until you land on the next (scale) step. The activity offers predictability in the repeating descending scale and its associated tonality. It also offers freedom in the in-between spaces.

Babbling – seeking the unknown

Developing babbling can serve two purposes, one personal and one social. On the personal level, babbling stretches the limits of the sounds a person is comfortable making. Stepping past your comfort zone into new territory is a brave act, and it is what improvisers do, "to boldly go where they have not gone before." When you babble, you allow the sounds to just flow, rather than controlling your sounds every minute. It is truly an exploration into the unknown. What people discover when they babble can be a reservoir of emotion that was waiting to be expressed. See what surprises happen when you release control and just babble. On the social level, babbling permits conversation among people, whether or not they speak a common language. In general, real conversations start with the awareness of others and the intent to connect and communicate. So do babbling conversations, which use sound for the sake of sound, along with all of the aspects of social speech that are not language-based. These include eye contact, facial expression, and body language. Having conversations in babble-speak sounds like music, but it also serves as a way to practice some of the most important elements of communicating.

David Darling babbles – play what you babble, play what you move

When the late cellist David Darling taught babbling, it was as a path to developing higher levels of instrumental articulation. He encouraged players to babble and to match the energy of their vocalizing with the movement of their fingers, often rapid and wild. This was a creative use of play what you sing, where the babbling vocalizing was being matched to an invisible air instrument. As a next step, he asked players to move their fingers onto an actual instrument and change nothing – remaining in an unplanned, energetic, out of control state. He saw this as a pathway to learning control of fast playing – by purposefully playing faster than you possibly could control, and eventually having the finger skill catch up to the body energy. By presenting this as a game beginning with babbling, he removed any sense of trying to play specific notes.

Shadowing – empathy and attentive, intuitive listening

Shadowing is an exercise in active listening and empathy. Standing face to face, two singers try to match each other exactly, in real time. To accomplish this, they take turns, alternating who is the leader and who is their "shadow," going wherever the leader goes. When this activity is introduced, the suggestion is given to go slowly and help the shadow follow with eye contact and body language. The goal is to bring your shadow with you, not leave them behind or fool them with quick and unpredictable changes. The shadow's job is to lend their listening and their music making to the expression of the leader. When experiencing this activity, it is quite a powerful thing to hear your voice amplified by the way your partner doubles you. Some people describe a constructive merging where it is hard to tell whose voice is whose.

When we listen to a musician or a speaker, we follow their notes and their meaning moment by moment. How can we be sure we have taken in their message? If we can repeat it, exactly. When a person gives us a note to match, we jump in as quickly as we can. And if the person gives us a short melody, we can try our best to match each note just when we hear it, rather than waiting for the melody to end. In this exercise, we truly do not know what we are repeating. We are not waiting to find out the meaning, we are being highly unselfish and lending our voice to the statement of our partner.

Shadowing is a perceptually sophisticated activity. You are listening for the next note while echoing the previous note. The next note might be higher or lower, and we have to adjust to match it rapidly, without thinking. This develops a focused attention that involves pure imitation and not interpretation, as there is no time to interpret.

Shadowing is useful in a social context when you are playing in an improvising group and you hear a partner playing something that you like, but their instrument is soft in the overall combination of instruments. You can help make their part louder by shadowing the notes. As is the case with play what you sing, shadowing is an activity that is best started simply, with short melodies that change notes very slowly.

When you are being shadowed by a partner, you experience support. Another person is literally "adding their voice" to what you are communicating. In your role as the model that others copy, the social task is to keep your sounds simple enough to be followed, and complex enough to be interesting.

Fugue form – imitation and repetition

Fugue form is like a round. When a player offers a rhythmic melody, the next player tries to copy and repeat it. The third player repeats what he or she heard from the second player, and so on, until the melody has passed through all of the players. Of course, not every repetition will be perfect, and the pattern may morph as it moves through the circle of players. Then the game resembles "telephone" with whispered messages that change in humorous ways. The job of every player is to support the melody as they heard it, while the first person has the honor and privilege of creating an original melody. It takes maturity and focus to repeat what you hear, especially in a complex sound environment. It requires zoning in on the essential element of communication from a partner and ignoring distractions.

In the Fugue activity, once the players have passed around the initial melody, they engage in the constant play of murmuring, making sounds and actively seeking a new and interesting melody to pass around. Eventually a new big idea can emerge. It gets "caught" by the players, passed around the circle and repeated with variations. The game becomes: share a big idea, murmur, catch a new big idea, murmur. All of the time in between clear melodic ideas is filled with melodic murmuring, much like the way actors in crowd scenes murmur interactions that have no words, but sound like background dialog. All the while the players are engaged in active listening with a constant influx of potential new ideas.

Steady State – find the common pulse, set yourself apart

Any way of adding contrast will make a musical contribution. The Steady State activity provides a simplification of what constitutes improvising and allows a player to contribute small changes in a repeated pattern. The rhythmic musical skills are: find the pulse of the music, match the pulse, create accents in the pulse, and change the accents. The melodic version: play a simple melody in regular rhythm, repeat that melody as a loop, and make minimal changes in the melody, such as changing a single note, or adding or dropping a note from one repetition to the next.

Reliable rhythm is one way of establishing a home base of security. Steady State helps beginning improvisers feel safe by making their task very simple – keep a pulse, play a very few notes as a repeated loop, and every now and then make one small change in the pattern. This change can be adding a note, so a four-note pattern becomes a five-note pattern, or dropping a note to make it a three-note pattern. The effect of this small change on the overall rhythm of the music can be profound. The lesson is that improvisation does not have to be complicated to be impactful. In the Steady State activity, all of the participants are sharing a common pulse, no matter how long their patterns are. Having a consensus about the pulse is the social agreement that makes the variations workable. Steady State, by virtue of its predictability and repetition, can be trance-inducing and hypnotic. In this state of listening, the small changes can be very powerful in altering the perception of the melodic figures.

Stately Dance – complexity from simplicity, the power of one small change

Improvising melodies in public can be daunting. One way of simplifying the task is to have a game that involves playing only one note at a time, and changing that note only when your turn comes around. This is very slow improvising. However, the Stately Dance activity illustrates how much of a powerful influence any one person's change can have on a group or community, sometimes for the better and sometimes not. In this game, the group agrees at the start that they will each play a very simple rhythmic figure, each on their own independent note. The game gets its name from the signature rhythm – short-long, short-long, short-long. At first, there is one note sounding. Then the next player enters, exactly matching the rhythm of the first player, but adding a new note so there is an interval sounding. The third and fourth players enter in turn, building a chord or tone cluster. When the turn comes around to the first player, the first player changes his or her note. This changes the harmonic context for all of the players.

The Stately Dance game is based on a group consensus – they agree to all play the same rhythmic figure, at the same tempo, each repeating one and only one note, and limiting their improvising to the simplest change. Just shift the note to any other note, one player at a time. In the course of creating these ever-shifting tone clusters, the players experience social context. The harmonic meaning of each note changes when a new note is introduced, and an old note is replaced. The group experiences dynamic diversity. While they focus on rhythmic unity, they experience unplanned harmonic tensions and resolutions.

Sirening and Chromatic Playing – artfully covering up our errors

Improvising requires some bravery. We enter into playing situations that are unknown and unpredictable. We search for our partners in a free improvisation through a wilderness of sound. We take a step and there may or may not be ground underneath us. Improvisers need some self-rescue skills that can get us out of any awkward position we may encounter. When we learn to play chromatically, using all of the half-step notes in the octave, we make it simple to save ourselves from any improvising missteps. If we do not like the note we played because it does not blend well with our partners, we can move along chromatically until we find a more suitable note. Such a solution is most often only one half-step away.

We can also save a misstep by repeating it and making the tension of the note an established feature in the music.

For voices and instruments that can siren continuously climbing or falling notes, the process is the same, but without the limitations of scale steps. We can bend our notes until we blend better. Either way, it is useful to approach improvising with an attitude of respect for exploring the unknown territory. We can say to ourselves and to our partners, "there is dignity in risk."

Play What You Sing and Sing What You Play – the path to fluency

Expressive fluency comes from being able to take internally heard melodies, rhythms and harmonies and manifest them in sound using voice and instruments. The voice is often the most immediately available conduit for expression. Fluency is learning to link the inner impulse to create a melody with the outer motor skills to control sound making. The practice of play what you sing and sing what you play addresses this linkage directly. Although this is a solo practice, it is a pathway to fluency that enables players to express their musical selves better in social settings.

Music improvisation starts with the impulse to make sounds. That impulse can come out using our voice, our body, or any instrument. Of all the instruments, our voice is the one most intimately connected to our body and our breath. Our voice expresses who we are and how we are feeling all the time. When we sing a single note – an "ahh" or an "ooh" or a "yay!" – we are expressing something personal about our feelings, and we are communicating emotional information to others, even when there are no words involved. What is in our hearts is given breath, and it becomes the vibrations of our vocal cords. We show ourselves to world by singing. Young children make vocal music easily as part of natural creative play. But children tend to get less free and more constricted as they get older and become more concerned with how other people may be judging them. They sing in private, perhaps but not in public for fear of ridicule. Undoing these fears is one of the most important things a music educator can do to promote creative expression. This can be done with relentless encouragement, and by modeling playful vocal explorations using call and response.

To develop fluency on an instrument, one can certainly benefit by learning scales and mastering famous pieces of music. This is an "outside-in" approach. Unfortunately, this does not foster original sounds and personal expressions of emotion in music. For that, we need an "inside-out" approach. That's where "play what you sing" comes in. When you play what you sing, you are developing the automatic links between the impulse to express emotion in song and the skill to produce that song on an instrument using your fingers. Here it is also wise to start simply. Sing a note and hunt for it on an instrument. Sing another note and hunt for that note. Sing a short melody and find the matching notes on any instrument. With time and practice, this skill becomes fluency of expression.

Play something familiar in a new place – the exotic hiding in the commonplace

This activity is mainly for solo exploration. Its purpose is to use the patterns of well-practiced and previously learned music in brand new ways by physically relocating the fingers on the instrument. A pianist shifts their hands a few inches to the left or right, and a different set of intervals and notes comes out, both familiar and different. A guitarist shifts the fret hand from open position to some place up the neck. A drummer shifts from the heads of the drums and cymbals to their stands and hardware. Something important and vaguely recognizable is preserved in keeping the rhythms the same, but the melodies have been transformed.

This is a remedy for playing too much like an automaton. Much music, especially intricate and difficult music, is practiced over and over so it becomes automatic. This helps the player get through a long piece, with practiced fingers that know where to go. But in the process of over-learning, sometimes the listening suffers, and the player loses the ability to "stop and smell the roses," or appreciate each interval and phrase along the way. Moving the hands to a new place creates unexpected results and re-invigorates listening. So does playing the piece in other new ways, such as extra slowly.

Conceptualizing Harmony as a Social Emotional Learning Skill – abstract imitation

What skills does a player need to have in order to respond to a musical partner by adding harmony?

Harmonizing is a sophisticated musical skill, although it comes easily to some players and is difficult for others. To harmonize a known melody, the player must comprehend the melody in a harmonic context. Melodies imply the keys they can be heard in, but that implication is not ironclad or universal. The intent of the original melody maker is invisible and the same melody may be given very different harmonic interpretations, many of which are logical and well-formed. Hearing a melody in the same harmonic context as the originator is a form of empathy. But instead of simply repeating the melody in unison, the harmonizer makes that invisible implied harmonic intent audible. And in the process, they enhance the melody and close the door on alternative harmonic treatments. A harmonizer hears what isn't there and makes it appear.

Harmonizers do not need to know what they are doing or how they are doing it. Harmonizing can be done intuitively. The ability to name the harmony comes when musicians study music theory and develop the vocabulary to describe the harmonic implications of melodies.

When Social Music Improvisation workshop leaders model harmony and conduct basic harmonizing activities, they are demonstrating how to be of support to a playing partner by hearing melodies in the same way the partner hears them. Most often the harmonizing will be simple and conventional. The melody will be harmonized in socially and culturally expected ways. And when those expectations are violated? There is the opportunity to hear new possibilities and contexts, even in an old familiar melody. And sometimes the alternative harmony offerings will be too much for the listeners to accept, and the harmonizer will get the feedback that not all innovation is socially welcomed.

Joining a free improvisation – being an adept musical conversationalist

To be a good improviser, there are three skill areas to master – being a soloist, serving as support, and knowing when to be silent. The solo role includes having access to feelings and telling a relatable story in sound. It also includes allowing your voice to be heard and controlling the inner voices that might be judgmental or inhibiting. Soloists are not just lone wolves; they also use their solo voices to support and interact with the musical statements of their playing partners in conversation and collaboration.

The path to becoming a bold and sensitive soloist involves developing instrumental fluency. The practice of "play what you sing, sing what you play" is tremendously valuable in achieving this end. Boldness also comes from taming the inner critic and taking the risks needed to gain experience. If the overall community values risk-taking and disavows snarky critiques, players have only their own critic to tame.

When serving in the support role, the most important skill is listening. It takes discernment and fluency to comprehend the musical statements of your partners and contribute to the mix in a sensitive and coordinated way. Supports include some of the skills mentioned above, such as providing a drone or a bass line. Or holding down the pulse or the rhythm by playing drums (or playing your instrument or voice as if it were a drum). The pulse is the lifeblood of rhythmic music, and the rhythm is the heartbeat. Support players can also lend their voices to the statements of their playing partners by shadowing and adding volume to a musical statement that could use boosting.

In the context of improvising, silence is more than simply not-playing. Silence can be creating space for a soloist to be heard clearly. It is a selfless act that serves the overall music. Silence can be active listening, since the opportunity to contribute can arise at any time, and your sounds may be just what is needed in the moment. It could be a harmony part, or an answer to a musical question, or a change of direction when the music needs one. Players change the overall sound when they strategically drop out of an ensemble. One way of creating contrast and interest is to change a quartet to a trio, or a trio to a duet. This is addition by subtraction. And on the other side, the player contributes again when they re-enter and the group grows rather than shrinks.

The Social Emotional Learning aspects of the major Rhythmic Connections activities for Social Music Improvisation

The main activities of Rhythmic Connections (as presented by Mary Knysh) are geared toward school-age audiences and take place mainly in K-12 public schools as assembly and residency programs. As such, there are classroom management details that deal with the logistics of getting large groups of children into a novel music-making environment. There is a predictable amount of initial excitement and chaos, and the challenge of the leader is to channel that energy into the music in a way that allows personal expression and permits the creation of a group identity through coordinated listening and interacting.

The overall goal of these sessions is to shepherd the students to increasingly artistic and integrated musical forms, based on their capacity to improvise in a socially responsive way. The sequence of the sessions generally moves from a *greeting* to a period of *listening*. In the course of guided listening, they *connect* with each other, and what emerges are musical forms that they spontaneously *create*. The next level of social interaction involves conscious and purposeful *collaboration* based on the forms that started as improvisations, leading in the end to "keepers," or musical pieces that they can *share*, reflecting the inspirations and cooperative processes they experienced.

The activities incorporate both rhythmic and tonal elements. In general, individual emotional expression is carried in the melodic and tonal activities, and group bonding and coordination is carried in the rhythmic activities. In the end, the two are integrated to produce a socially coordinated expression of meaningful common emotions that individuals can relate to.

Me and We – the audible sounds of diversity

When students make their own sounds, all at once, it can be chaotic. On the other hand, the sound of students each making their own individual sound is an expression of diversity and inclusion, so long as the activity is presented with an emphasis on experiencing the energy of the resulting sound, rather than judging the sounds or the people who are making them. We would quickly grow bored of music that was too predictable. The interesting aspect of the One Quality Sound activity at the core of the Me and We game is that the more times a group makes their own sounds together, the more coordinated the sounds become, even when the instruction is to stick to your own sound without "sweetening" it or adjusting it to match your neighbors. People crave both diversity and harmony, and it is reflected in the gradual coordination of the sounds they make, even when they have permission to make any sound they wish.

Me to We – the sounds of coordination

When the task is to quickly come to rhythmic consensus, the students are challenged with choices for how to participate. The task requires both structure and persistence on the one hand (even stubbornness), and flexibility and selflessness on the other. To come to one rhythm out of many individual rhythms, some of the players have to be stalwart timekeepers, maintaining their own rhythm as a beacon for other players to notice, match and navigate towards. But if everyone took that approach, there would be chaos. Some of the players have to sacrifice their own rhythmic contribution and take up the rhythm of someone else, for the good of the group and to better coordinate the overall sound. It is the sound that does the teaching in this activity, as the students can tell if they have reached a place of agreement, or if there remains more than one rhythm competing for the minds and hands of the group. After the group has reached consensus, it is possible to ask the students which role they chose and what challenges they experienced. If the purpose of the group goes beyond music making, the discussion can include where else these same choices – to stand up for oneself or to surrender individuality for the sake of the group – occur in their lives.

Rhythm Sticks – partnering in a shared pulse

When we give students in art classes blank paper and crayons or paints, we allow them to fill the resulting space however their imagination inspires them. In this partner rhythm activity, we give the students four beats of blank time, and challenge each pair of students to come up with a stick pattern that fills the available time. These patterns reflect both the cooperation within the pairs, and the diversity and individuality of expression that shows itself in the variety of patterns played among the pairs. The variations in sound that begin as inherent and unconscious elements of sound making can become the focus for verbal discussion after the sound making has been done.

When the players meet each other in duet activities using sticks and boomwhackers, they practice pragmatics of communication. Their "hellos" in sound have the same purpose as handshakes and are prone to the same excesses and adjustments as when we are greeted with a hand that feels like a limp noodle or a vise grip.

Musical Home – evolving a sound for tribal identity

The Musical Home activity is a process of expansion/exploration and contraction/honing that results in a group creating a "signature" rhythm that represents its own creativity. In the first phase, individual creativity is encouraged via simple spontaneous rhythm patterns. At the group level, the infectiousness of the patterns that come from certain individuals leads some of the patterns to be adopted and gain power and momentum, much like any idea that "goes viral." The individuals have the freedom to create, and the group has the freedom to choose among the creations. When the students make their choices through listening and imitating patterns they like, the selection process takes place in the music itself, rather than through verbal lobbying or votes that might confound popularity with magnetism. People are drawn to the pattern that becomes the group sound. They do not automatically choose the one that originates with the most popular student. In the cacophony of group music making, each person's contribution is anonymous. The emergence of a sound that expresses the tribal identity, based on an implicit group wisdom, comes from the appeal and the quality of the musical idea alone. Often, the ideas need to find their most simple, basic and accessible form to gather the group into unison play. From this refining process, the emergent rhythm grows in its power because it reaches all of the players.

One Sound Around – spontaneous spatial compositions

Many musical activities demand skills that come from technical practice – to play music in tune and in time. This group activity pares down musical contributions to one sound, which levels the field so that no specific prior musical instruction is required. In place of melody, harmony or rhythm being the intentional units of music, the medium for this game is space, as the sound moves around the circle in dynamic and changing ways. The resulting music is incidental, and the emphasis is on the readiness to respond to an immediate social signal to pass the sound along, reverse its direction, or toss it to a receiver across the way. The students practice immediate focus on a split-second signal, and also focus on the body language needed to let a partner know which signal is being given.

Breath to Boom – synchronizing in sound and movement

Self-regulation presents particular challenges to younger students. Their energy levels and moods are transparent, but their age-appropriate impulsivity makes group music (and other activities) more difficult to coordinate. Breath to Boom incorporates the self-regulating power of slow intentional breathing (Breath) in an activity that also permits happy discharge (Boom). When the discharge is done in a socially coordinated manner, the resulting sound has a crispness that is immediately noticeable and self-rewarding.

Balloon Breath – toning and sirening to achieve a unison sound

This activity teaches relaxation breathing, combined with tones that siren from high to low and low to high. With repetition, the group learns to all end on the same tone and hold a unison pitch.

Babble/Freeze – learning order via chaos

There is a paradox in teaching. Sometimes you have to allow chaos to practice coming to order. Without its opposite, order is a less clear concept. To practice self-regulation, this game first has students babble and gesture energetically. They exercise self-regulation on the word "freeze!" and try to stop their sounds and movements all at once. The sound will give them feedback as to whether they were successful in stopping as a group.

Heartbeat – focusing using a group pulse

This is an imitation game that begins with the students tapping their hands in a common steady pulse. The sound of all the hands tapping at the same pace will reinforce the oneness of the group. The leader gives patterns to follow, and the hands move from laps to chest or from head to floor. The group has verbal cues to follow from the leader's description, and also visual cues from the peers' actions. The sound is most coordinated when everyone follows the cues together.

A group finds the holes in the sound to create a groove.

Ways to Join a Group Improvisation

Solo	Social Support	Foundational Support	Contrast
Start a conversation	Imitate	Provide a drone	Drop out and return
Tell a sound story	Echo	Provide a pulse	Find the holes
Use authentic emotion	Answer	Play a looped melody	Fill a hole in the rhythm
Use what they give you	Shadow	Play a looped rhythm	Play higher or lower
Represent your home base	Harmonize	Offer a chord progression	Offer something new

Join a group improvisation by contributing a musical idea for others to build around, or by supporting the ongoing rhythm and tonality of the group. A player can make a positive impact by offering contrast, and through conversational interactions that come from sensitive listening.

Part Four -
Teaching with Flow: Facilitating and Sequencing Social Music Improvisation

In parts one and two, we described the main activities that prepare students to improvise spontaneous music in solo settings, in small ensembles, and in larger groups. In part three, we showed the social emotional aspects of these activities. In this section, we turn to the leader's role, presenting improvisation both as content and as an approach to teaching.

Let's consider a continuum of spontaneity when teaching. On one end, there are presentations that are entirely pre-planned. A lecture, a demonstration, or a theater piece can be precisely timed and scripted with no options for variation. Next, there are presentations that have a set sequence of agenda items, but there is some flexibility in how much time is spent on each item, or there is a Q and A period when unexpected questions can be addressed. On the more flexible and spontaneous side, there are teachers who use a checklist rather than a set sequence, and they craft a different path through their material every time, as long as they eventually cover all of the items on the checklist. Lastly, there are presentations that are dedicated to emergent content, in which the checklist or curriculum items are addressed only when they appear in the interactions with the students, and very little of the sequence or content is teacher-initiated. These various approaches reflect individual teacher's styles. Some students are more receptive to higher levels of structure, and some gravitate to higher levels of spontaneity, if given the choice. When the content of the class is improvisation, it stands to reason that welcoming spontaneous and emergent events is congruent and consistent. The more tools teachers have that permit them to be facilitators and guide the flow of experiences in their classes, the more flexible they can be, as needed. In the end, all teaching approaches can benefit from some level of receptiveness and adaptability.

One can approach teaching improvisation as an improvisation, with preparation and spontaneity. Just as members of an improvising ensemble approach a blank block of time with receptiveness and boldness when they create music from silence, listening and technique, facilitators can approach their role in a similar way, using activities and interventions like notes, harmonies, contrasts, and silences. These are the principles and facilitation strategies I have been applying in college level classes in music improvisation.

Every teacher/facilitator comes to their classes and workshops with a "bag of tricks" of activities to present, but even a great collection of separate activities will not automatically create a smooth flow from one activity to the next. Linking, "flow," and other elements of sequencing are separate skill sets from presenting specific isolated content.

For background reading on this approach to teaching consult the following resources: for instrumental and vocal music, Music for People (main resource books: Return to Child by James Oshinsky and Innovative Drum Circles by Mary Knysh); for drumming and rhythm activities, the Drum Circle Facilitator's Guild (main resource book: Drum Circle Facilitation by Arthur Hull); vocal ensembles using layered loops and solos, Circlesongs as taught by Bobby McFerrin and his associates (main resource book: Vocal River by Rhiannon). These resources are described in detail in the annotated bibliography. See page 110.

When we improvise music, we look to create a flow between one phrase and the next, to tell a story and communicate emotion, and to support the stories and expressions of our playing partners. When we teach improvisation, we can craft experiences for our students/attendees that can take them through a flowing sequence of activities. When the depth of learning depends on keeping students engaged, how we extend their active participation matters. We can do this with the artful linking and sequencing of activities.

We will be presenting some examples of how flowing sequences can operate in the teaching of music improvisation for ensembles and soloists. It is important to emphasize at the outset that the examples we give here are not meant to be literally replicated. The philosophy we embrace is that the teaching of improvisation can be done as an improvisation and will unfold uniquely every time it is presented, flexibly and organically, in ways that meet the needs of both the students and the facilitator. It is not important to teach exactly the same way twice, even if you are teaching multiple sections of the same class. The content is better described as "being authentically true to the moment." If you have done that each time you teach, you have given your students the essence of improvisation.

In seeking an answer to "what might come next?" there are a few useful principles to keep in mind that can help keep a teacher or facilitator in a receptive mindset, picking up cues from the group's process, while also following one's own inspirations and, if applicable, also following a plan for delivering specific content.

The Main Principles of Using Flow – Strategies and Mindsets

Use what they give you

Scenario: you are starting a session at a music improvisation workshop for adults. The room has a piano in one area, a large circle of chairs that incorporates the piano, and a sound system with a wireless microphone. As you enter to size up the space, there is a group of participants around the piano, jamming. They are taking turns soloing over a jazz standard.

You have a variety of tasks to accomplish in getting your session off the ground: you need to help the participants who are just entering the room orient themselves as to where to sit and what to pay attention to; you need to establish yourself as the facilitator of the session so that when you direct an activity, the group follows your instructions; you need to make all of the participants feel comfortable, including the ones that are currently playing. What do you do?

Here is one possible solution: First, signal the group clustered at the piano to keep playing. By doing this, you are establishing your leadership – they are now playing because you have asked them to. Your next direction to them may be to modify their playing, or stop, but they now will follow you.

Use the mic and body language to orient the new people. Adjust the chairs so they form a circle no more than 5-10% larger than the number of people you expect. Remove any excess chairs and position the remaining chairs so that people will be close enough to hear each other easily.

Find a role for the "rest of the circle (ROC)." In this case the ROC will be everyone who is not in the group playing near the piano. If the group is playing a sophisticated tune with complicated chord changes, the ROC can most readily join in on mouth and body percussion. Have the ROC take on the sounds of a drum kit – brushes on a snare, sticks on a cymbal or high hat, bass drum pulse or rhythm, and occasional fills or flourishes. You can do this by modeling the sounds yourself and asking the ROC to imitate you, and then do it their own way. If the tune is well known, you can have the ROC sing long tones that go with the melody. If possible, subdivide the ROC to sing long tones in harmony. A group of singers that are harmonizing long tones can function like a string section or a wind section on a recording. You can conduct the singers to dip and swell their volume levels or you can start and stop the singing to mimic the way a horn section "hits" its stacked harmonies in rhythm.

Alternatively, you could invite additional players from the ROC to join the group around the piano in the role of featured soloist. You would need to know the skill level of the players you invite to not over-stress anyone or put them in a position beyond their ability.

Be Sensitive to Natural Transition Points

When a piece has ended, there is an opportunity to step in as facilitator and guide the group to the next activity smoothly. Timing is everything. Step in too soon and you are diminishing what may still be in the process of ending. Step in too late and you encourage mild chaos, such as side conversations, checking phone messages, and other reflections of disengagement.

In the class or workshop setting, let's say a small ensemble is finishing its improvisation. For the purpose of this example, envision a class with 30 total participants having just listered to a 3- minute improvisation by a quartet of players. As the group is ending, the facilitator can be thinking – "what kind of energy might follow this group?" "Does the entire ROC (rest of the circle) need to be immediately involved, or do they have the focus and patience to listen to another small ensemble right now?" and "Do we need to deepen a mood, or go for a contrasting mood?"

You could let the group that is playing finish and let a short period of silence "bracket" their piece. If your decision is that the whole group will now play, you can cue them to be ready by using large gestures that everyone can see. When you use exclusively body language gestures and not spoken instructions, you are not "breaking the spell" of silence and flow.

Cue the Next Group

If you intend for a new group to follow the first group, you need to decide the composition of this new group and prepare them to be ready to play before the first group has come to silence. No later than 30 seconds before the anticipated ending of the piece, make clear eye contact with the players you wish to have in the next ensemble. Use hand gestures to cue them to be ready to go on your signal. Be decisive and clear about exactly who you are selecting; you may need to move about the room somewhat to have straight sight lines. Be unambiguous as well as kindly in your gesturing. If flow is your goal, try to avoid selecting players who have logistical needs - nothing kills momentum as much as plugging in, tuning up, or moving across the room. Electric instrument players and pianists can easily be incorporated into the flow by inviting them to be the players in a segment of class that takes place near the beginning, when there is an expected transition from milling about to starting up.

You can create smooth transitions if you engage the whole group in a warmup, then segue into your teaching content via call and response or modeling. Next sculpt the group in half for a continuation of the activity and continue subdividing until you reach the desired size for your breakout group practice. You can also showcase the smaller groups one at a time. The groups get their practice with the players that are in their last subdivision, and you have not interrupted the flow by counting off or using a verbal process to create small groups.

Creating Flow Using Changes in Group Size

Sometimes an activity works with groups of different sizes, and the facilitator can keep energy flowing by transitioning through various combinations. One can sequence from working with the whole group to half the group, and then to pods of three to six people (sequencing from large to small) or one can build from duets to quartets to half the group and end with the whole group (sequencing from small to large). These transitions also have the effect of being a social mixer, allowing changing interactions among the participants as they recombine in new ways. You can present varied content in this fashion, from stepping in rhythm to vocal harmonizing.

The key to recombining subgroups is to keep an activity going while shifting partners. The participants always feel connected to at least one group. For example, the group is stepping to a common pulse. While stepping, they are asked to join a common drone, then harmonize the drone note. Next, they are asked to turn to a partner and hear their unique combination of notes. After a minute or so, they change partners. But both the pulse of the stepping and the underlying drone note provide continuity through the transition. After a few such duets, the group can be asked to form quartets, sample these more complex harmonic combinations, then change partners into new quartets. These quartets can be individually showcased by fading down all but one group at a time, with a return to "everybody playing" to create the groundwork for the next transition.

Another important element in maintaining flow and interest is to keep introducing novelty and contrast. Duets, quartets, and octets all sound different from each other, and different from the whole group. If you employ drum circle principles while sculpting, each player remains engaged and active while the subdivisions are taking place. This is very different from the "dead air" taken up by creating subgroups if you have the students count off or receive a group assignment of A/B/C/D etc.

Let's say you have set up a vocal activity involving four subgroups. Each subgroup is singing a different part that they were assigned and allowed to modify as they "make it their own." To transition from the four groups each doing something separate back to a whole group, introduce movement. Have the groups mill about and interact while continuing to sing their individual parts. They will experience their own parts quite differently as their auditory field changes, getting further from the unison cluster of their home group as they interact with new people representing different rhythms or different melodies and pitch registers. After milling about and interacting, have the players reform a new circle.

The transition from getting settled to active listening

When you want to begin a concert as a listening event, and the concert is staged in a traditional way, the audience has many cues that something important is about to happen. At T-minus five minutes, auditorium lights flash to alert people to take their seats. Closer to the start time, the house lights dim and the stage lighting begins. Ambient music fades to silence. An attentive audience participates in the silence and helps create the ground against which the music will stand out.

The flow from "audience milling about" to "audience is engaged in listening to a concert" is aided by these cues.

But when there is no supporting staff of house managers and lighting or sound personnel, how can you, alone, as a performer or presenter, create and establish a similarly intense atmosphere for listening? After all, the music is as much in the listening as it is in the playing. Many excellent performances are missed by audiences who were not quite prepared to listen and appreciate what was being given them.

Recognizing and channeling chaos

Before any musical event, the audience is in a state of relative chaos. I don't mean gross disorganization; but there are hundreds of separate side conversations and foci for people's attention, from the written programs to the theater décor (not to mention the distractions of cell phones). The same holds true in smaller venues, from a coffeehouse to a classroom. The goal of the performer or instructor is to move the audience from multiple and private foci of attention to a single shared focus on the presenter or presenting group.

In drum circle facilitation language, there needs to be an "attention call," a clear signal that "something is about to happen, so pay attention." An emcee's introduction is one such call; "Ladies and Gentlemen, tonight we are proud to present ………!" And if there is no emcee?

I was recently at a workshop given by master singer and composer Bobby McFerrin and his colleagues who teach an ensemble improvisation form called Circlesong. There were 150 attendees in a large hall. There was a stage, but no curtain and no emcee. The morning's first presenter was there to facilitate a whole group warm up that would get everyone moving their bodies, everyone warming up their voices, and everyone cooperatively and attentively interacting with their peers. What she did to transform the room from 150 individuals, each in their own private worlds to a coordinated group looked like this: she stood on the stage with a microphone in her hand. She quietly began singing a short, simple melody, repeating the phrase over and over. With patience and insistence, she continued presenting her sound until more and more people in the group joined her. Eventually (but fairly quickly), the whole group had transitioned from a crowd milling about to a focused ensemble, standing still, facing the stage, and singing what she was singing. A seamless transition.

She used the initial song to gather attention, so the melody was simple and the energy was gentle. From this, she transitioned into a warm-up that involved the body, the breath, the resonant chambers of the face, and the articulation muscles of the mouth. A full, sophisticated vocal preparation warm up. But it did not come across as instructional; each activity was presented as a guided invitation. The relaxed manner made it easier for people to get immersed in each activity, without worry that they were doing it wrong.

Emphasize contrasts

Flow is the opposite of stagnation. A facilitator is sometimes needed to nudge a group out of playing patterns that have become stale and repetitive. The experience is re-enlivened when the facilitator steps in and highlights new things to listen for. For example, if a group is in the middle of a jam and you step in and conduct changes in loudness level, the group is reminded to do this on its own after you step out of the facilitation role. Similarly, if you sculpt the group to emphasize instrument groups with specific timbres (all the shakers, all the acoustic guitars, just the flutes, etc.), the group will better be able to pick those timbres out in the overall mix of sound once they resume playing in a self-regulated way. And the easiest and most profound contrast is between sound and silence. If you initiate a stop cut, the group does not just stop playing – the sounds and rhythms remain in auditory memory, vividly. They are continuing to listen and to have a shared listening experience even in the silence. Music educators call this ability to hold music in active short-term memory "audiation." Bringing the group back in to the groove after a stop cut is an experience in bonding – the contrast highlights the coordination and cohesiveness of the group.

Covert Teaching and Automatic Learning – unattended dimensions

Whether it is called "scaffolding," "layering," using a "platform," or any other term, each musical activity, once it is securely accomplished by the group, can serve as a backdrop for a new activity. Rich music often has multiple elements occurring simultaneously. We are all able to be drummers and singers at the same time. When we hold a steady drum beat as a group and listen for calls to respond to with our voices, we are using what some psychologists call "an unattended channel." The drumbeat gets carried in an automatic and un-reflected way, building body memory, much like we can ride a bicycle and look at the scenery at the same time.

Consider the following musical activity: four players are sitting in a circle, chamber music style. Their instruments are capable of sustained tones (think bowed strings or woodwinds, but the activity is adaptable).

The rule of this game is simple - you have one rhythmic figure to play, and it has to be on one note only. All players play the same rhythmic figure.

The first player starts. Let's say he or she plays a single note in the rhythm: short-long; short-long, etc. as an endless loop. When the second player enters, that player adds a new note, so there is an interval sounding, in rhythmic unison. When the third player enters, that player adds another new note, so there is (potentially) a chord sounding. When the fourth player enters, there is either a chord or a cluster sounding.

Now it gets interesting.
When it gets back around to the first player, that player changes his or her note to any new note. This changes the harmonic context of all the other notes. The same is true when the second, third and fourth players change their notes, in turn. All the while maintaining the same coordinated rhythmic figure.

After a few rounds of this game, the players are set free to turn the piece into a free improvisation.

What musical skills have they been practicing?
Which of those skills were learned because they were focusing on the dimension of that skill, and which skills were learned because they were not putting much attention into that dimension?

The activity can be presented as an exercise in rhythmic unison and precise articulation, with lesser emphasis on the changes of notes. In that case, the players focus on rhythm and choose their notes automatically. Yet they are experiencing harmony along with rhythm. Sometimes the channel or dimension that gets less conscious attention is learned by the body in a different and deeper way.

As another example of an unattended channel of learning and practice, consider this situation: A facilitator has a group keep time by walking in place. To the pulse of the walk, the facilitator sings out rhythmic "calls" and the group echoes the calls back in rhythm. What is the attended dimension? Echoing the call. What is the unattended dimension? Holding the pulse in the body.

The Main Strategies of Teaching with Flow

Purpose	Intervention
Get started	Start with an attention call and a clear, focused rhythm or melody
Channel chaos	Turn rhythms to rumbles and conduct dynamics, endings, and transitions Conduct melodic tone clusters using dynamics and sculpting Repeatedly cut the sound by half Conduct crescendo and stop cut
Use what they give you	Welcome opportunities to build a lesson from serendipitous events
Natural transition points	Anticipate and cue the next group in advance
Create contrasts	Change group size: whole group – half group – pods
Emphasize contrasts	Sculpt to highlight differences in instrument timbres, musical styles, loudness levels, moods
Host the party	Provide chord progressions to invite solos and blending Start strong rhythms for the group to join with and layer over Provide a simple melody to invite harmonizing Invite the audience to join in and participate
What to avoid	Dead air and periods of talking Stagnation
Include movement	Types of movement: move to music, stretches, incorporate mingling as part of an activity
Ways to end	Big finale, stop cut, layer out, fade to silence Trickster ending: call and response, withhold the last call

The "bag of tricks" of the well-prepared facilitator, ready to create flowing sequences of musical experiences.

Skills of the Well-Prepared Facilitator

Be ready to play chord changes for the group to blend with and solo over

Some class experiences are for subsets of the whole group – the activity calls for a sequence of quartets to play, or a small group is momentarily featured. There is always a challenge to keep the rest of the group listening actively when the participants are not directly involved in the music making. One way of engaging the whole group after a period of passive listening is to offer a repeated set of chord changes that invite harmonic bending and melodic exploration. If you are an experienced piano player or guitarist, you can do this yourself, using chord progressions and rhythms that are more calming or more energizing as needs be. But if you are not able to play a chording instrument, then what? You can have prerecorded "loops" of chord progressions available, although the mechanical aspect of the recording may be an issue at times. But if you are good at using your sound system, you will know when to strategically fade out the backing track and let the group experience their unaccompanied music and their own creations. If your group includes reliable players who are familiar with chord progressions, you can request that a participant lay down repeated chord changes, freeing you to facilitate without having to tie up your hands and your position in the room.

Be ready to start strong rhythms for the group to add layers to

Sometimes you may decide the best transition is not to a melodic/harmonic activity, but to a predominantly rhythmic one. In the example above, the facilitator provides a chord progression – hopefully with reliable rhythm and the right level of complexity to invite the group to join in, and neither bore nor overtax their instrumental and listening skills. Similarly, it is helpful for a facilitator to be a good enough drummer to provide a strong and sustained groove on the kinds of hand percussion that invites the group to join in. To be heard over a large group of players, it is useful to have drums with a penetrating and deep sound, such as a surdo, dun-dun or djembe. Leading while drumming, however, presents the same challenges as leading while playing piano or guitar in that the leader's hands are occupied, and any other conducting has to be done with more limited body language or with words. If the group is able to sustain listening at lower volume levels, then the facilitation can be done with quieter and more subtle percussion, such as a shaker or bell. Leading with body percussion and vocalizing percussion sounds provides more options and sources of contrast, as well as being a good transition to "sing what you play," and the reintroduction of melody through singing.

Whether you are improvising or teaching an improvisation class, a useful guiding principle is "commit and adjust." If you offer a rhythm on a hand drum, you are trusting that the other players will find ways to jump in. But if by any chance they did not, you could turn the drum pattern into a solo and then morph into another activity.

Here is a common example of transitions that support the key Music for People practice of Play What You Sing and Sing What You Play. Start with the whole group drumming (1,2, Let's All Play!). Transition to drumming with vocalization of the drum sounds. This is the essence of Sing What You Play in which each person's voice is following and tracking what that person's hands are playing. Drop out the drumming and you have transitioned to exclusively vocal percussion. Let the vocalizing go on long enough to inspire variations. Then have the players match their vocal sounds on their instruments. This is the essence of Play What You Sing, in which the instrumental playing is meant to imitate, duplicate, or shadow the voice.

Be ready to start strong melody lines that can be repeated and harmonized

Sometimes the choice of transition is to an activity that allows for harmonic exploration. If you offer a simple melody line, without any chord arrangement, you are leaving space for the group to invent its own harmony. A favorite simple melody that David Darling often used was the opening phrase of "Jingle Bells." It begins on the third degree of a major scale, so it was a useful jumping off place for teaching harmony. He would have the whole group repeat the phrase as a loop, then model singing a harmony part below the melody, which he would then pass along to a subset of the group. Next, he would model singing a harmony part above the melody, and then pass that part to a third section of the group. At that point, the group was singing "Jingle Bells" in three-part harmony.

Involve the audience

Anytime the whole group is not actively playing, there is a distinction to be made between the people singing or engaged in making music on their instruments and the rest of the circle (ROC) who are, for the moment, idle. The ROC is sometimes in the passive role of being an audience, and they are at risk of becoming disengaged if left in that role too long. Involving the audience can take the form of incorporating them as a large pipe organ, singing drone notes that complement the portion of the group that is actively playing. Or one can invite the ROC to be the rhythm section using mouth percussion sounds. In between one listening segment and another, a leader can initiate a call and response or the activity called Sah (singing in unison, raise a note up a half step and back) to engage the ROC long enough to renew their patience for hearing additional small groups.

Limit questions and verbal analysis; keep the music coming

And now, a brief word about announcements, dead air and energy drains. At every workshop or class, there are key pieces of verbal information to impart. These may involve assignments, logistics, meals, transportation, or schedule changes. No matter how important the content, announcements interrupt the flow of musical listening. It is a worthy challenge to balance informational and musical experiences.

In general, a good rule is to limit announcements to two minutes or less. Put key information in posters that have large enough fonts to be easily read by multiple people at once. Another option is to distribute information via downloadable pdf files. Again, fine print tends to require more effort to read; make the most important details large, distinctive, and attractive.

If you choose to make verbal content announcements and you don't want to "buzzkill" the listening experience, try embedding your announcements in a rhythmic call and response activity. This way, your verbal information takes place in a "cool down" period that remains musical.

Set up a pulse or a rhythm on body percussion – hand claps, and lap or chest drumming. Conduct the volume level down so you can speak and be heard over the rhythm. Give a few melodic or rhythmic calls so your audience is attentive and engaged. Then cue them what is coming next, for example, give a call: "I'm gonna tellya." The group will answer: "I'm gonna tellya". The next call might be: "how to find the lunchroom" (answer: "how to find the lunchroom"). Call: "it's through the double doors" (answer: "it's through the double doors"). Call: "and then the second left" (answer: "and then the second left"). The whole group now has a body memory of identifying where the lunchroom is. While it takes practice to become adept at phrasing your information to fit in cadence in a call-and-response format, it is definitely worth learning.

Another way of maintaining an atmosphere of musical listening is to make your announcements over a group drone, or with a soloist playing musical snippets in between your pieces of information. For the drone, you can always use the Music for People "Sah" activity, where the whole group drones on one note, and creates contrast when they are guided to slide up or down by a half step or other interval, and then back to the home note. The speaker can conduct the volume of the group down to a level where the announcements can be heard over the drone. In between bits of information, the leader can sustain interest by using different intervals in the "Sah" game, or by inviting harmonies or soloists. The goal is to have the activity be familiar but not overly predictable.

Too Much Talk

Once the leader shifts from musical facilitator to imparter of verbal info via talk or lecture, some bad audience habits can emerge. Some people will think "the musical part of the session is over" when the music making stops, so they may feel free to pack up, move about, and otherwise distract from the focus on the verbal information. Presenting the information in a musical form makes it clear the session is not over yet and keeps everyone's attention.

Talking can also trigger more talking. It is common for some participants to want the opportunity to ask questions or make their own announcements about travel needs or self-promotion of events. Maintaining a musical setting minimizes the opportunities for other people to elongate the talk time or sidetrack the session to a personal agenda. At every event there may be a need to communicate about such things as lost items, ride shares, and events of general interest, but plan ahead – having a designated poster area for such things will keep the info out of the listening atmosphere you are trying to establish.

Breathe/release is a legitimate activity

Sometimes as a leader, you need to stall for time. You may still be sizing up what direction to go in next, but the activity you were facilitating has ended and the group is looking to you for the next one. David Darling used a movement, inspired by Tai Chi, in which he put his hands on the top of his head, gestured upward and outward, while saying "aaaaand … release!" while taking a deep breath. He was sometimes encouraging the group to breathe, relax, and focus together in silence. But at other times he was stalling until he could think of what to do next with the group. It did the group no harm and most often they thought he was offering a worthwhile lesson.

Let people move

If you are a dancer, then you likely have a good internal sense of how much sitting around is tolerable before you need to reenergize, stretch, and move. Even great playing and singing needs to be bracketed with opportunities to move the whole body, not just the music- making parts. If you are not a dancer, try to be mindful of the need to move and work in whole body activities in every half hour of class time. Standing up for a vocal melodic improvisation or a body percussion activity can serve as a re-energizer. Activities in which the group mingles while making music helps the group members become familiar with each other, exposes them to each other's sounds, and serves as a physical energizer.

End with a drone or rhythm that keeps going

If an activity does not have to end in silence, end it with an ongoing sound such as a drone or a repeated rhythm. It is much easier to modify an existing group sound than to "restart the engine" and get a group into a coordinated activity from scratch. This also will give you time as the facilitator to reset the layout of the room, choose specific players or equipment, etc., without there being "dead air." In Drum Circle trainings, there is a tradition of facilitators taking turns leading the group. They always end their sequence of facilitation by having the group return to an ongoing groove so that the next facilitator has an easier time stepping in. They call this practice "jump time."

How to use silence

Some experiences will naturally end in silence. In many ways, the depth of the listening experience will be reflected in the depth of the silence. Such silences can be shared. To keep the flow of the overall class going after such a silence, have the group do something physical together, in silence. The simplest such activity is to breathe, or to breathe and make a gesture of "release," inviting change and openness to something new. Having the next ensemble or activity staged will make it easier to transition from silence back to sound. However, if that is not the case, the "go-to" activities that will work to bring the group back to sound are: call and response, body percussion, vocal drone, Sah (drone, move up or down, return to original note), modeling a common rhythm using shakers, or imitating shakers with voices to establish a pulse.

Artful ways of ending a teaching segment

All good things must end, even to make room for more good things. The ending of a group improvisation experience might occur spontaneously with the group recognizing and capitalizing on a natural ending. But sometimes a group gets stuck and needs to be guided to an artful ending, or time constraints require a transition.

A facilitator can create an end that also serves as a heightened listening experience. Simplest of all is a fade-out. This can be conducted to happen in stepwise fashion, reducing the volume by half each time until there is only the subtlest of sounds. The most dramatic end is the stop cut. The facilitator can add to the drama and build suspense by leading changes in volume and creating false endings (stop, audiate and resume) before the big finale. The group can come to an end by "layering out," with people dropping out one by one based on their seat location, or their instrument category, or the specific sounds they are contributing. The group can be brought to strategic chaos – a drum rumble or a mixed-instrument cacophony – before a powerful unison stop (think of the ending of the Beatles' "A Day in the Life").

Matching the sounds of your partner.

What exactly is flow?

I had the privilege of learning about flow from master teachers. In the 1980s and 90s, cellist David Darling developed a set of music improvisation activities and a way of presenting them that embodied the best of music education. His activities were accessible and useful at all levels of musical sophistication, from beginners to professionals. His demeanor was disarming, humor-filled, and relentlessly encouraging. And he had a knack for chaining activities together seamlessly, like an FM DJ (in the era before podcasts) might string together an hour of continuous music with no distracting talk or advertisements.

David allowed me to study his approaches, and he reflected on his own teaching in some of the essays we published as part of the *Return to Child* book that Music for People uses in its improvisation training program. Interested readers can go to the "Shadowing David" section of *Return to Child* for the most detailed breakdown of David's teaching style. It is unfortunate that he did much of his teaching in the era before cell phone cameras made video so ubiquitous. But there is an outstanding 3-CD set, *The Darling Conversations*, in which David and composer Julie Weber discuss his work, and a few workshop videos that are searchable on the internet. The organization that David founded trained hundreds of teachers in this model, chief among them Mary Knysh, who transitioned from trainee to co-leader to main teacher when David retired. Mary has contributed much to improvisation education, especially in the area of sequencing activities and keeping all participants active and engaged.

When one thinks of a "teacher," the common image is of a person at the head of a classroom, standing while the students are seated, imparting knowledge through words, provocative questions, engaging lectures or problem-solving tasks. In laboratory learning, students are turned loose to experience physical and chemical processes for themselves. A teacher is needed to verbally instruct the students in what to do, what to look for, and in some cases, how to stay safe around fire, chemicals, and electricity. But in the lab, experience itself is one of the main teachers.

The model of a facilitator is fundamentally different from that of a teacher. A facilitator seeks to create experiences for the students with a minimum of setup. The means of engaging the students is through infectious activities that are self-motivating. The aim is for students to learn by doing and reach relatively high levels of sophistication through listening, social responsiveness, and ultimately, self-regulation. A facilitator guides with as light a hand as possible. While the learning experiences can be profound, to an outside observer the activities can look like games. Making learning fun deepens rather than cheapens.

One could lecture on the roles a person can play in a group improvisation – to be the soloist, the person providing harmonic, melodic or rhythmic support, or the one who contributes to contrast by being strategically and attentively silent. Or one could create opportunities for students to improvise together and have them discover these roles for themselves by noting what makes some improvisations exciting, dynamic, and interactive, and other improvisations more static and less interesting. *The vocabulary can follow the experiences rather than introduce them.*

Studying Flow

For many years, my role within Music for People was "scribe." I watched how David Darling, Mary Knysh and other leaders ran their sessions. I took notes and worked out a shorthand system (similar to the one Arthur Hull uses in the Village Music Circles facilitator training program) to capture the nouns and verbs of facilitating MfP sessions. The easiest things to see were the activities – the whole group is walking in place; the group is divided into quartets, the leader does call and response, etc. The subtle things took longer to conceptualize – what were the specific calls that the leader gave? How did those calls incorporate the musical concepts that the leader was going to expand on as the session progressed? I noticed that call and response is a worthwhile activity for its usefulness in emphasizing listening skills and imitation. Its whole-group format makes it anonymous and generally non-threatening to participants nervous about making mistakes. It is also a great way to create an "overture" for a session, where the participants get subtle practice at the same skills the leader will introduce later on. For example, if one of the activities in the workshop is slated to be "solo over a descending scale," it can be useful to give the participants experience with a descending scale by incorporating it into the calls. This is the heart of experiential learning – the participants don't need to know that they are singing a "descending scale," they are gaining experience by imitating the model that the facilitator provides with his or her calls. Later on, the leader can label the concept "descending scale," but only after the participants have lived through the experience of it.

I was fascinated with the sequences that embodied "flow," and it was also obvious when flow was interrupted. Talk generally killed flow. This was hard for me to accept for a long time, since I was very interested in understanding and analyzing processes, and it was helpful in a training setting to provide some feedback in words to the trainees. But what I had to learn was both patience and memory. To capture what happened when, the shorthand symbols were a great help. Then I had to learn to wait until the group was ready for a break from making music to take up the "let's look at what happened" process. In keeping with a supportive way of operating, we often asked "what worked, what needs work, what would you do differently, and how did it feel?"

Yea! energy singing.

Part Five –
How to Practice Flow (for facilitators and teachers in training)

The Leading Lab challenge – a "Card Game" for developing sequencing skills

In the formative years of Music for People, we presented a challenge to leaders-in-training: we asked them to find a way to link together three random activities from the Music for People teaching blocks (*Return to Child* activities) without relying on verbal instructions, and with one activity flowing into the next. The activities were written on index cards, and leaders in training picked three cards from the deck. In the puzzle below, try to connect the dots in one continuous line. Similarly, sometimes it is necessary to go outside the box and add an activity or two to create a smooth flow.

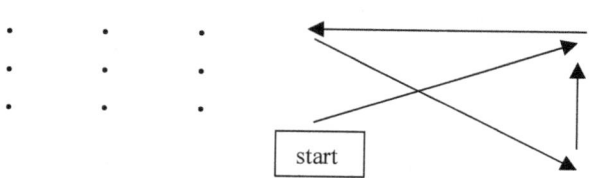

For example, how would you link the following three activities/content areas?
  A) Solo/drone (with a partner, play a short melody and hold the last note); harmonizing in thirds; even-handed drumming
  B) The importance of silence and space; Yea! energy; using a descending scale as an accompaniment for improvising solos

The use of cards made for some very random combination of activities; these were useful challenges to push the creativity and resourcefulness of the trainees. In common workshop situations, these activities might not be juxtaposed. Most often the activities in a teaching segment will have a coherent theme. But it does no harm to be ready to present any combination of activities.

Combination A): find a way to present Solo/drone, harmonizing in thirds, and even-handed drumming.

Rhythm is a very useful skill area to start a teaching segment. Getting the group into a common groove helps solidify the group rapport and bonding. To start even-handed drumming, I might begin with the room pre-staged to have a hand drum at every seat. Start by modeling a strong, simple rhythm, and invite the group to join in however they choose to. After a few minutes of letting the groove get established and "simmer," I might move my own drumming into an even-handed "go-do-go-do-go-do" quarter note pattern with no breaks or accents. If I use gestures to invite the participants to mirror me, many will, and some may remain on contrasting rhythms. If needed, I might speak the drum syllables out loud to get the whole group drumming even-handedly.

From here, there are many drumming variations that could be introduced. But to focus on evenness, I might model playing just the right hand for a while, then just the left, and invite the group to listen deeply and strive to make the same sound with either hand. Then we can return to even-handed drumming while alternating hands, and then to another drum jam. After the new groove is established, I can give a vocal call over the groove and invite an echoing response. I can signal for the group to loop or repeat the vocal phrase over the ongoing drumming. I can then ask the whole group to continue drumming and ask half the group to also continue the vocal phrase. Then I can give a new vocal phrase to the other half of the group. If my goal is to introduce singing in thirds, this new phrase will be a harmony part, the same melody moved up a third. Now the group is drumming and singing in harmony. I can reinforce the listening to harmony by bringing the group to unison singing on either vocal melody (original or harmony) and switch the groups back and forth between the two parts multiple times. Having established the concept of singing in thirds, we can repeat this activity with a new melody and harmony and add contrast by cutting out the drums and singing a cappella from time to time.

Lastly, to bring the group energy back down after energetic drumming and singing, I could bring the drumming to silence and bring the singing to a continuous drone. Over this drone I could invite a few soloists. Next, I could ask the soloist to end his or her solo on a new drone note and ask the group to join (quietly) the new drone. Lastly, I might invite two experienced players to demonstrate solo-drone in duet format, fading the group drone out so the duet is all that remains.

This sequence is workable and flexible; all three activities are covered, and the introduction and sequencing of the activities is done with a minimum of verbal instruction and no down time. If this group session were followed by a break-out period, the participants would have three distinct new skills that they might work on in the smaller group context.
Combination B): Find a way to present the importance of Silence, Yea! energy, and using a Descending scale

Yea! and Ooh energy is one of the first contrasts taught in Music for People sessions. Yea! is the energy of a cheer, a warning, or an exuberant shout. Loud, fully embodied, and sincere. Ooh energy is the tender energy of a lullaby or a prayer. It is tender and passionate, whether it be joyful, comforting, poignantly sad, or plaintive. I might begin a sequence with call and response using both Yea! and Ooh timbres for the calls. If I offer calls in a predictable rhythm, the group will be taking in that underlying pulse and putting it in their bodies based on the repetition. I can have the group loop/repeat one of the calls. If I plan well, one of the calls will be a short descending scale segment, such as CBAG. I can slow the loop down so there is space between the notes, then mark the rests or spaces with silent gestures. I can change the rhythm so the people to hear the CBAG phrase in both 2/4 time and 3/4 time. Using a gesture to mark the spaces or rests in between the notes gives the opportunity to invite a soloist to play during the spaces. As the descending scale pattern repeats, we can have some of the repetitions filled with soloists and some left silent. I could also stop cut the group and have them experience silence that is filled by maintaining the pulse or maintaining the scale phrase internally, then bring the group back to the beat by counting them in. If you try imagining how you would link these activities into a sequence, you are likely to come up with your own creative variations.

The point is that seamless sequencing and linkage is possible with literally any three (or more) improvisation activities. The emphasis for one leader might be whole group inclusion, for another person the emphasis might be on drawing out more expressive solos over a looped pattern or a drone. No matter what the content, the manner of presentation can feature seamless flow from one activity to the next. There are a few collateral benefits to this approach. For one, there is often an "unattended dimension" of practice. In the first example above, while the group is both drumming and singing melody lines in call and response fashion, the group is actively attending to the new melody – this is necessary to recall and repeat it. They are not attending to their own drumming, which goes on simultaneously, automatically, and unconsciously. That is a deep practice, like riding a bicycle while looking at the surrounding scenery. Presenting activities that flow one to the next also maintains high energy and engagement among the participants.

Listening is the most important of all musical skills.

Part Six -
Teaching K-12 Public School Music Educators to Use Flow

Starting With the Conclusion

The culminating activity of the college improvisation class I taught was always an all-improvised concert. Most concerts at this school have a set program of written music that is rehearsed all semester and advertised to potential attendees. Not this one. Every piece was a spontaneous creation. The students had two aspects of improvisation to address in the concert. First, they were participating as improvising musicians, ready to offer a solo and support their playing partners with the musical elements of melody, rhythm, harmony, contrast, and silence. Second, they were also collaboratively improvising the sequence of the concert program, using principles of contrast and flow. The students were aiming to lead and facilitate at least three activities each, and to chain together more than one activity in their role as leader. They were free to play in as many ensembles as were suitable, but they were strongly urged to participate in no less than half of the program.

The act of faith for the improvisation concert was to plunge into group improvisation armed with the willingness to see what happens. The students most often discussed the format of their opening and of their closing, but not the note for note content of any of the pieces. They might decide one year to open with a percussion procession into the hall, inviting audience participation from the outset. Another year the first activity might be a chamber music-style improvised ensemble. Or an opening that involved playing over chord changes to give all the players a chance to warm up a bit. To be sure, during the course of the semester the group had ample experience in all of these formats of improvised music, but there was no pressure on concert night to re-create any piece that they might have done before.

Some years the students did employ a "cheat sheet" to remind them of their options if there was any temporary lull when deciding, intuitively, "what comes next?" That cheat sheet looked like this:

Where to Start	What to Balance	Specific Ideas
Splash	Be strategically silent	Shadowed duet with soloists
Layer in	Remember the lawnmower	Instrumental quartets
Call and response	Imitate, answer, converse	Sculpted percussion
Pass out parts	Shadow, harmonize	Improvise lyrics
Use what there is	Support your partners	Play over chord changes
Chord progression	"Yes, and" … make them right	Contrast: whole note/half note

Where to Start	What to Balance	Specific Ideas
Bass pattern	Play what you sing	Morph percussion to vocal
Ooh and Yea! energy	Offer a pulse, a line, a groove	54321 game
A-B-A form	Offer a pedal tone, a drone	Found objects, non-instruments
Rhiannon quartet	Move out of your seat to where you are needed	Add humor – squeaker trio
Sculpting	Group size contrasts	
Soundtrack to a picture	Involve the audience	

Of the items above, a few may need explanation. "Remember the Lawnmower" is a motto about leadership. Once the lawnmower is started, you do not have to keep pulling the cord. Whatever you inherit becomes something you can use as your starting point. It is a reminder to not take on the pressure to do too much, and to use what the previous activity might have given you. If one activity ends and the audience enthusiastically claps, you have the opportunity to harness the clapping, conduct the audience to continue clapping as a rhythm, and use that as the pulse for the next activity. This is important because when students are first learning to lead activities, they tend to think in an atomistic way, considering one activity at a time in isolation. With this mindset, every activity has a start, a middle, and an end. But in practice, the activities within an improvised concert or workshop are like the cars of a train that can be assembled in any order. There is one actual start, or locomotive, and everything that follows can be linked to what comes before and after, optimally in a continuous flow.

The "Splash" is the vocal version of One Quality Sound. The students conduct each other to sing a random sustained tone cluster. The Rhiannon Quartet is a vocal improvisation structure with four roles: one person sings a repeating groove, another person sings a complimentary groove that fills holes in the rhythm of the first groove, the third person harmonizes groove 1 or groove 2, and the fourth person is free to improvise solo over this platform of sound. Whole/Half was a minimalist game that two percussion students invented. They each played marimba and kept to a common pulse, playing either whole notes or half notes.

The students were reminded to use contrasts in group size: solo, duet, trio, quartet, half group, whole group, add the audience; and contrasts in group composition: just the right side of the audience, just the left side, just the men, just the women, just the friends, just the parents, etc.

The concept of moving out of one's seat is very important in improvisation, especially with un-amplified instruments. For example, in a typical improvisation class with mixed instruments one might find a violin, a saxophone, and a marimba, but also a ukulele, an upright bass, and a piano. These instruments have very different volume levels. In practice, for these instruments to function as equally important members of a group, the players need to regulate the volume levels to "support the weakest member." One of the ways of making a quiet instrument more salient is to change its placement in the room. If the ukulele player cannot be heard over the concert grand piano, it is possible that the pianist is playing too loud. It is also possible that the ukulele player is too far from the piano to be heard, and since the ukulele is the more portable instrument, the easier and more practical adjustment is for the ukulele player to come near the pianist. This applies to any soft instrument playing among louder ones. While the goal is to achieve a blending that benefits from the timbres of all of the available instruments, the intervention to get to that optimal blending may depend on the more portable quiet instruments moving closer to achieve a sound mix.

Moving out of one's seat is also necessary at times to get the attention of a player who can be lost in personal musical reverie. Improvisation sometimes leads to entrancement, in which players lose track of time and their fellow improvisers. To bring such a dreamer back from their dream, it may be necessary to move close enough to them to establish eye contact.

Year after year, students who began as novice improvisers and facilitators created an engaging program of spontaneous music on the fly. They used the principles of flow to craft sequences with resourcefulness and contrast. They included the audience as their accompaniment, providing a drone or a rhythm section. They played from their home bases and musical histories, whether that was Argentinian folk music, show tunes, gospel, rock, or tap dancing. And they had fun that was infectious. How did they get to this level in one semester?

I remember how they began.

Reconnecting with the joy and playfulness of music-making

These students did not all come into my class, after three and a half years of the undergraduate music curriculum, believing in their own inherent musicality. Some among them entered class with so much respect for written music that they were afraid to play a "wrong" note. This fear of being wrong can severely limit anyone's ability to experiment and learn by doing.

I know how important it is to develop technical competence in music - to master reading, breath, muscle control, phrasing, intonation, and timing. For most players, that requires a lot of persistent practice and dedication. But there is another side to music making that is expressive and spontaneous; one that is passionate but not weighted by criticism and judgement. It has the exuberance of discovery and creativity and connection. This is the aspect of music that often draws children into an interest in an instrument - to *play*, not *work* at music. Bringing people to a playful mindset can't be done by talking to them. But if they are led into experiences that are engaging and disarming, people recover their child-like enthusiasm and riskiness or friskiness. There is no set formula for creating such experiences. What works for one teacher may not work for another. Yet there are some general principles to follow. Be authentic, be positive and encouraging, and maintain a balanced focus between your prepared ideas and what is happening in the room in the moment. The latter is always going to be the more important priority.

Being open to what is spontaneous in music and in teaching does not come without dedication and preparedness. What I want to communicate to students is not gravity and seriousness, rather it is encouragement and approval. When an inhibited student makes a sound, I celebrate the step taken towards freedom of expression. When a student is brave enough to chain together a handful of notes as an unplanned solo excursion, I want to be the first to say, "You did it!" I am well aware how fragile the egos of adolescents can be, and for all of the trappings of their teacher certifications and degrees, college students are only just ending their teenage years. Many are immensely talented, with bold and practiced voices, and with a repertoire of instrumental pieces that they have prepared for "juries" and concerts. Nonetheless I am interested in accessing the inherent musicality that dwells in them when they are unpracticed, just going about their day, and humming while driving, walking, or bathing. Putting them back in touch with their ability to be spontaneously creative and to be surprised by what they create. In short, "returning to child."

How can we encourage and nurture openness in music students?

First, it helps to be a model of authentic expression in music. I strive to embody my conviction that spontaneous creativity in solo and ensemble improvisation can be the most natural thing in the world. To encourage students exploring, it helps for me to be a bold and humble explorer, and to model what I would like to see from them. That means I solo honestly, taking risks and recovering from glitches if they occur. It means when current events trigger deep emotion, as when the Cathedral of Notre Dame in Paris burned, I played the emotion that was moving in me at the time, and asked them to do the same, based on their experiences of loss.

Second, by making the class improvisation experiences accessible and safe enough without being trivial. Sometimes the whole world of music can be expressed in one moment of authentic emotion. The priority is not to play certain notes - it is to share the human story that the notes convey. We include activities that are expressive of the whole range of human emotion, so long as it is honestly felt and put into sound. We want the class to bond as a supportive group that welcomes being real. Providing safety while encouraging risk is a balancing act that continues to have expanding horizons. We start with simple activities in which each student is propped up by joining an ongoing ocean of group sound in the form of soundtracks, drones, rhythmic grooves or loops, and chord progressions. These accompaniments are gradually withdrawn until students can stand on their own, soloing unaccompanied, or being, for the moment, the only soloist within an ensemble. As the class builds trust with each other, these risks naturally deepen over time.

We welcome honest errors. You can't know how without learning how. I can't insist that a student start at the endpoint of being competent in a new skill. To help soften the bumps of the learning process, there are "cover up" skills that all improvisers learn along the way to make the best of their inevitable errors. To repeat a note is to give it the ring of the familiar, even if it was initially unintended. This is a way of applying the philosophy of "use what they give you" to oneself - you can use your own errors as building blocks. Your unexpected clinkers provide musical tensions to take advantage of as long as you keep playing. Another good "cover" is to develop skill playing chromatically, whether in stepwise fashion or with sirening and rote bending. This allows a player to quickly get to the note they intended, even when it is better late than never. You are never more than a half step away from a note that will work, and often no one is the wiser when you say, "I meant to do it that way."

Start with listening. Communion with the muses of musical creation is to be entranced in deep listening. Students may need to learn to listen meditatively, to put aside inner and outer distractions, and quiet the common busyness of their minds, if only for the time we have class together. Listening is one form of worship in the temple of music. Listen with reverence.

Use the body to get to states of relaxation and inner listening. We often incorporate movement into our warmups, from stretching to mingling. We want to l ve the music with the whole body, not just the music-making parts. I see the disconnection when students first try their hand at leading rhythm activities. There are so many things to focus on. Students can feel pressures that distract them from being present with the beat in their bodies. They can be concerned with success or failure, fear of peer comments or faculty judgements. They can be overfull with plans and ideas without a clear plan for how to sequence and set up their next step from the current activity. Sometimes the most important feedback I can give a student is to step in time to the rhythm and to put the rhythm in their shoulders, h ps, arms, etc. This not only helps the student lead more organically, it also helps their students follow their rhythm.

The Pallet of Choices for Teacher/Facilitators

Let's imagine that you are a teacher and you are facing your first improvisation class. What do you need to notice about your group that will help you craft activities that are suited to their playing and listening level? These observations will also serve you when you are in a more temporary role as a facilitator among your peers.

First, assess the capacity of the group to listen to each other. This is impacted by maturity, room acoustics, and the mix of instruments present. A lower capacity to listen means you will need to emphasize more basic activities and it may require more frequent facilitator intervention.

Second, assess the consequences of chaos. In an adult group, chaos can lead to quieter playing and more intensive listening, as when a drum circle deteriorates into a train wreck with unclear rhythmic centers, and the group reorganizes on its own. However, in groups with less maturity, chaos can bring more chaos and require relatively strong interventions to stop all activity and reorganize based on the facilitator providing structure, as when children leave the lunchroom for the playground. That is, their gravitation towards chaos is natural and enjoyable, but it goes counter to having a single coordinated group focus. If the impact of chaos would make it very hard to restore functional order (and get the feathers back in the pillow), then the facilitator has to keep a closer watch on the level of group listening.

Third, assess the mixture of instruments present and their tonal possibilities. Instruments can be played in both standard and non-standard ways. Guitars can be played as scratchers with the strings muted to emphasize rhythm and percussion sounds. Tube shaped drums can be played with a hand in the bottom, somewhat like a French horn, to modify the bass note and create melodies. Drumsticks can be used to click each other as well as to beat a drum.

Among the most important things a facilitator can do is to open up the group to their own sonic possibilities. The group may not have experience combining the less common instruments in their midst, but the facilitator can sculpt the group in ways that highlight the softest instruments, the most interesting sounds, the possibilities for juxtapositions that have humor, and so on. Once the sonic options have been exposed, the group is free to use them as they self-regulate their sounds.

A few words about piano – special challenges to hear and see peers

When one of the instruments in the ensemble is a large or loud piano, the placement of the other players is important because of two fields - the visual field and the sound field. A pianist may legitimately have a hard time hearing players that are on the far side of the piano's main body. The players would hear better if they situate themselves at the side of the piano or close to the keyboard, so there is nothing but open space between their instrument and the pianist's ears. However, the pianist's natural field of vision is towards the keyboard. I often position the other ensemble players within 45 degrees forward from the pianist's right side to optimize sight lines and make nonverbal communication easier among the players. A glance, a nod, or a shared breath all help the players be in sync and stay aware of opportunities to share solo space or end together.

Over the years I have taught improvisation, most of the students who are music majors come to the class with some training on piano, even if it is not their main instrument. They all have experience reading for right and left hand and for playing prepared pieces, well enough to pass their keyboard class. Given this history of experience, I was often surprised that the students could not easily sit down at the piano and play simple chord progressions that invited others to play along. What was missing in their prior instruction?

To confess, I am not a trained pianist. I am a terrible reader, and I have never had to master and perform a piece of music for piano, although I have played for audiences (as part of a band) on guitar, bass, piano and hand percussion. But I have been a bold explorer of the piano since childhood because there was a piano in the house and my playing was tolerated by my parents. I was fascinated by the mechanisms of the pedals and springs, the unexpectedly long keys and the various hammers and felts. I loved the depth of the sound that would resonate when the dampers were lifted, echoing not just piano notes, but every nearby vocalization and clatter. As a child, I learned "Heart and Soul," "Chopsticks," and some nameless ditty that used mainly the black keys and had words that were double entendre. As a teenager, I had a guitar teacher who taught me music theory on piano, where the note relationships were easier to illustrate. My ear was trained to identify intervals and transpose pop songs into any key. This has proven to be a far more valuable lifelong musicianship asset than I would have guessed at the time. I became adept at playing chord progressions common to pop music, shifting them to any key, and making them interesting by providing a bass line in the left hand and articulating a chord with suspensions and snippets of melody in the right hand. My college students who were not trained jazz pianists could not do these things.

Nuts and Bolts of Basic Piano to Accompany or Lead Improvisation Activities

Use basic chord progressions that emphasize common notes or long tones. When a person is first learning to improvise, they appreciate simplicity and safety. Chord progressions that have clear common notes shared between consecutive chords are a good starting point because they limit the likelihood of stumbling on a "clinker." A player can hold a note while the chord changes and experience a new harmonic context for their held note.

Another simple structure is to play chords that shift over a held drone in the bass. The home note in these situations is always clear. As an example, finger an A minor triad in the right hand and play an A note in octaves in the left hand. Set a pulse with the left hand at a slow marching tempo. Play whole notes in the left hand and half notes in the right (right hand is playing on 1,2,3 and 4; left hand is playing on 1 and 3). Or you can syncopate the left hand and play on 1 and 2-and. Keeping the left hand constant on the octave A notes, descend with the right hand, keeping the same chord shape, one step at a time, using just the white keys. From the ACE triad, the next chord will be GBD, followed by FAC, etc. all the way down the scale. This progression keeps the minor mood and ends with the diminished BDF before returning to A minor. For added drama, you can modify the BDF to the diminished 7th BDFG#, or the dominant 7th BDEG#. The point is, this progression is physically simple, and it invites long tone improvisation in A minor.

What if the group you are working with includes mainly Eb or Bb brass or woodwind instruments? You would benefit from learning the progression above in C minor or G minor.

While there are many tonally sophisticated songs in pop music, many famous songs have no more than four chords, including the bridge. In any key, play the I chord followed by the V chord, and then the VI minor chord followed by the IV chord. Play this in any consistent rhythm, fast or slow. There are literally dozens of songs that follow this exact pattern. The comedy music group the Axis of Awesome chains them into a medley in their act:

> Elton John – "Can You Feel the Love Tonight" (from The Lion King)
> John Denver – "Take Me Home, Country Roads"
> The Beatles – "Let It Be"
> Bob Marley – "No Woman, No Cry"
> Avril Lavigne – "Complicated"
> Eminem featuring Rihanna – "Love the Way You Lie"
> The Cranberries – "Zombie"
> Natalie Imbruglia – "Torn"
> (and more than 20 others)

When a leader plays a chord progression and invites students to improvise melodies, some of the improvisations will be inspired by tunes that the player remembers. Using known tunes as part of improvisation has a long history in jazz and rock music. The iconic guitar solo in "Sunshine of Your Love" begins with the melody of the song "Blue Moon." Eric Clapton quickly turns the familiar notes of that old song into a bluesy exploration. That is, he plants the seed of something familiar, then "goes off the page" and inserts novel and spontaneous improvising.

The only other progression I can think of with an even longer list of song titles than the "four chord song" would be the 12 bar blues - I IV I I IV IV I I V IV I I.

Since these blues chord changes are so broadly used in blues, rock, and country music, it is very useful to offer them as an accompanist to encourage improvisation in familiar music formats.

A-B-A form in songs

Why do songs have bridges? While some songs are exclusively constructed around a single repeated chord progression, other songs break up the predictability with a separate section that could be a song on its own. For example, in the Beatles' song We Can Work it Out the bridge is in a minor key with a descending scale structure, while all the verses are in a major key. In Paul Simon's Still Crazy After All These Years, the bridge modulates to a new key, as does the instrumental solo.

When a facilitator is leading a chord progression activity from the piano, it is always allowable to throw in a "B" section or bridge. To avoid losing the group when initiating this change, you need to lead the group into the new "feel" of the bridge, possibly by emphasizing the bass notes and walking the bass line into the chord change for the bridge.

Contrast is an extremely important musical element. Every change creates interest.

Social music involves cooperatively sharing the tonal and rhythmic spaces.

Part Seven – Sequencing

How to seamlessly chain activities together for deep listening experiences

This is the crux of Social Music Improvisation teaching - crafting group experiences that are engaging, that present the content that the teacher has planned to deliver; that make creative use of serendipitous events in the group; and that enhance listening interest though contrasts in format, including changes in group size, prevailing emotional energy, degree of physical involvement, and degree of social interactiveness.

How to get sessions started

The dictator/professor stops whatever murmuring, side conversations, or musical interactions that may be going on, calls for the group's attention verbally and non-verbally, then tells them what will happen next and launches the next activity.

The facilitator looks for something that is ongoing in the group to expand on in ways that will eventually incorporate the whole group. If a subset of the group is playing, the facilitator might tell them to keep going to create a repeating pattern that the rest of the group can imitate or follow, and then the facilitator will look for ways to engage more and more of the group in the activity. There is usually no need to end whatever energy is ongoing in the room before starting the "lesson." The facilitator's skill is to redirect the group's energy in a constructive way. If a group has an energetic jam going on when a session is supposed to be starting, a facilitator can encourage the high energy, move it into a rumble (which is unsustainable and seeks a coordinated ending). The next step is to direct the group to end the rumble, transitioning into the next activity.

In the absence of a usable ongoing group interaction at the start of a session, most facilitators have a bag of tricks to get sessions launched. These include using soundtracks and rhythmic/melodic loops that the group can play along with, and the recruitment of "ringers" in the group who can be counted on to play repeated rhythms or chord progressions while the facilitator can give instructions and the rest of the group can interact and improvise.

Throughout a class, lesson or workshop, a facilitator is on the lookout for ways to integrate what the group spontaneously creates with whatever activities are predetermined to be on the agenda or curriculum. For example, I begin every class with a group improvisation as a warmup. To involve the whole group, on some days I begin with a rhythmic activity, and invite people to join a groove and be playful, trade solos, have musical conversations, sculpt interesting subgroups, and create dramatic stops and re-entries. On other days the group intro activity might be tonal/harmonic, starting with a repeated chord progression at the piano. This allows me to invite long tone blending, expressive solos, and harmonizing. I can capitalize on whatever interesting parts the students came up with to build layers and then conduct volume changes to create a mix, as one might do as a producer in a studio. If the group happens to have a good supply of vocalists, the opening warm up might be vocal, with vocal drones, harmonies, vocal rhythmic patterns, beat boxing, and the creation of layered vocal grooves to which volunteers could add lyrics from improvised or remembered songs. There is always a warmup, but the form it takes can allow for flexibility and spontaneous teaching moments.

Moving vocal patterns so they create chord changes

Whenever I present a warmup, I look for opportunities to transition to the next activity without stopping the music-making. If a planned lesson involves chord progressions, I might begin by leading the group into a groove that consists of layered melodic parts in a distinct key. As a first change, I might conduct the group to take the entire pattern up a half-step, then return to their original notes. This is the model for all chord change excursions - home - away from home - back to home. As a next step, I might bring the group volume down, sculpt the group down to only a few reliable singers or players, and model changing the tonal center of a pattern from the current home note to a fourth above. The smaller group will copy the change. I can then invite the whole group to make this shift together - home - up a fourth - back to home. If the group can do this in rhythm a few times, the next sequence to try is: home - up a fourth - up to the fifth - back to the fourth - back to home. I might hold up the number of fingers that correspond to the interval shift - four for a fourth, one for a half step, etc. Or I might use hand gestures that show horizontal planes in the air to signal the chord changes. Once a group can do this, they can improvise melodic patterns and use them to provide an impromptu a cappella arrangement for popular music tunes that have simple chord changes. A worthy and challenging extension is to also have a hand signal for a shift from a major to a minor key, without stopping their melodic patterns.

Here is another example of how to introduce the chord change activity above. Begin with Sah - the whole group breathes together, then sings a unison home note on the syllable Sah while placing one hand on top of the other. The leader models a change from the home note and home syllable - Sah modulates up a half step to "ey" as the top hand pivots open, and back down as the top hand returns. The leader can then request harmonizing without specifying who is singing what part or whether the harmony is major or minor. The group will work it out based on a gesture to create stacks of harmony (move the hands showing horizontal planes at various heights while modeling a harmony). Once the group is harmonizing, repeat the Sah modulation activity, with the whole group raising up a half step while changing the syllable from Sah to "ey" and back to Sah. Use larger gestures to change the excursion from a half step to larger scale jumps. Eventually these include a fourth and a fifth from the home note, sung in harmony. Then add a backing rhythm, such as a 12-bar blues shuffle or heartbeat. Conduct the shifts from the home note, in harmony, to the corresponding chords. From here, it would be possible to solicit a volunteer soloist to layer in, either vocalizing, singing a known song, or adding spontaneous lyrics.

To keep the joint emphasis on both improvising and teaching improvisation, I will ask for volunteers to try facilitating any of the activities that I lead. Our rule for sharing this role is to always exit the facilitator role with the group engaged in an ongoing activity - a melodic, percussion or vocal groove, or a vocal or instrumental drone. This allows anyone to pick up where the last facilitator left off and move the group into new places or let the group "simmer" and create its own next steps.

Naturalistic transitions

When producers put together an album of music by an artist, they have a problem to solve regarding the sequencing of the tracks. On the one hand, they want each track to stand on its own, since the tracks might be played in many different contexts. On the other hand, they want to concoct a listening experience that is a journey through all of the tracks. That journey might have a narrative storyline, or at least a trajectory of energy that starts strong and ends strong.

When facilitators of improvisation put together a program of musical activities, some of the same priorities apply. Each activity should stand on its own as a worthwhile experience of music-making and listening. And there should be a trajectory of energy through the fabric of the event that starts strong, ends strong, and moves from high emotion to calming/soothing and back. We avoid stagnation and repetition. One might recall the vaudeville truism: "never follow a banjo act with another banjo act."

Since the nature of improvisation is inherently unpredictable, there are only so many things a facilitator can do to influence the energy of each activity. If one piece involves the whole group, the next piece, for the sake of contrast and energy change, might involve a subset of the whole group. This can come about by sculpting selected players to showcase, by instrument category (drums, piano, voices, strings, guitars, brass), by likely music genre (rock, blues, jazz, classical), by location in the room (adjacent players), or by the compatibility of what the players have been doing within the ongoing whole group activity (make the shift by subtracting out all but the players you select to continue, based on their combination of rhythms, timbres, melody lines, or harmony - use what they give you). The sculpting can be hidden with the creation of pods of players. When the whole group mixes and forms small groups, wait until the group of desired size and instrument composition is present. The leader has done the selecting, but the group experiences what feels like a serendipitous process.

One thing David Darling used to do when he conducted an improvisation concert involving 50-60 players was to cue the next "act" while an activity was ongoing. A half minute before the transition, he would let a vocalist or pianist know he was likely to bring an activity to a close and pass the energy to them for a solo. He would keep a set of four empty chairs in the center of the group he was teaching. During any whole group activity, he could subtly fill the four seats with players. That quartet would be ready to take over as soon as the whole group activity faded down or ended. In the reverse direction, he was able to transition out of a quartet activity by gradually fading in the whole group, using a drone note compatible with the quartet's tonality, or by using a rhythm that mirrored the quartet's pulse or tempo

Platforms and Scaffolding - Creating Vibrant Sequences with Novelty and Safety

Structures that invite participation in improvisation by virtue of their predictability - drones and loops and chord progressions - can also feel stagnant after a while. These activities are not end points, but platforms to build on, layering and sequencing more varied activities, always returning to the home base of the predictable drone, loop or progression. When you transition away from a predictable activity and back, you offer both Safety and Novelty as contrasts.

A Chord Progression example: At the start of a session, the facilitator is at the piano. He or she plays a simple chord progression at moderate tempo. There are bass notes in the left hand and chords in the right, perhaps arpeggiated chords in rhythm. But there is no specific melody that the facilitator is playing. The melody space is left vacant to leave room for the players to fill it with their own ideas. The facilitator invites long tone improvisation by the group over the chord progression. This can be vocal or mixed vocal and instrumental. The group creates an ocean of sound with all the members improvising long tones in a kind of spontaneous harmonic soup. The facilitator next encourages melody lines. These melodies can be very short and simple, consisting of three or four notes. If any group members are singing or playing a particularly expressive or beautiful melody, the facilitator can bring down the volume level of the group and showcase them as a soloist. Among the choices for variations are: fade out all the instruments, including the piano chords, and experience an all-vocal group improvisation. Then bring the vocalizing to a single drone and introduce aspects of the "Sah" activity, modulating a group drone up or down a half step, or to other intervals and back home. Next, establish a vocal rhythmic groove in the key of the drone Then re-introduce the original chord progression in the same key, with the groove as a driving force. To add variety and complexity, highlight how there can be a shift in the tonality of the groove when the chords change. This can lead to a "song form" group improvisation, with changing chords. This in turn can invite improvised lyrics and so on.

A Drone example: Start with a group drone, and transition to a rhythmic groove and then to multiple layered grooves. The leader can pass out parts, but be sure to allow individual creativity "make it your own." Over this group rhythm, invite soloists. You can mix the group by having the participants walk around and hear the interaction of their parts. Then create pods of 4-6 people to jam together. Fade or stop the rest of the group to showcase one pod at a time. Lastly, reconstitute the whole group exploring rhythm. End the segment with a rumble, bring the rumble to a vocalization "buzz," turn the buzz into a drone. You have come full circle.

A Layered Parts example: The facilitator passes out a rhythmic melody line to the whole group. The next step is to signal 1/4 of the group to continue that groove, while the rest of the group is stopped. A new pattern is passed out to the adjacent 1/4 of the group so there are two parts going. Then parts are passed to the remaining two groups until there are 4 interleaved parts. These parts can be random, or they can be strategically chosen to highlight some aspect of teaching, such as harmony, polyrhythms, etc. Once the four parts are established, soloists can be invited to soar over the layers. Multiple soloists can interact in conversational exchanges. The groups can be released to make the parts their own. If new patterns arise in a given section, that pattern can be given to the whole group, and a new multipart structure can be built, either by one person passing out the new parts, one leader per section passing a new part to their section, or volunteer section leaders emerging.

The point in all of the above examples is that the initial structure of a drone, a chord progression or a rhythmic groove can be a temporary stopping place that more elaborate group improvisations are built on.

The Impact of Play

Recently I made a guest presentation in a nursing school class. Their course is called "Healing and the Arts," and my topic was group improvisation. I have been coming to this class once a semester for several years, and I usually bring percussion supplies to create a mixed ensemble of hand drums, beater drums, tambourines, shakers, wood blocks, and bells. The students this time around (and typically) consisted of 25 young adults in their early 20s, three of which identified themselves as musicians. However, when asked, the vast majority of the class acknowledged that they played an instrument or sang in chorus through high school. There is something odd going on that students with so much musical experience would not define themselves as lifelong musicians.

The students take to drumming in an improvisational manner very quickly. If I give them a pulse to follow, they jump in quickly, matching and creating variations in the pulse - subdivisions, accents, syncopations, and cross rhythms. I don't have to tell them how. Their innate musicality and social senses take over. Nonetheless, the student group is competent to connect but not tremendously bold in their common risk taking. They blend in more than they stand out. To get students to engage fully in the group rhythm, it has to feel like play, or they have to feel as uninhibited as children at play. This past session, in an effort to disarm the seriousness that can be an inhibiting force, I added a set of squeaky dog toys to the array of percussion that was handed out to students. The toys make sounds when you squeeze them, and it is simple to do so in rhythm. Not surprisingly, the level of exploration and the energy level of the whole group was elevated after the squeakers were introduced. What they did not realize is that the toys brought about an attitude of playfulness. That attitude is the key to higher levels of individual and group creativity, not the toys themselves.

Contrasts between drum circle improvisation and other forms of group improvisation

Some instruments can easily be highlighted at high energy levels, with the backing of a large group of players. An African drummer can often be heard above the level of a drum ensemble as he or she solos on a djembe. An electric guitarist is buoyed up by the density of sound provided by the rest of the rock band. Other instruments require modifications to the sound levels in order to be clearly heard. The jazz band pares down to just piano and drums to provide a sparse acoustic environment for the bass solo. A singer may need amplification to be heard over the choir unless the choir dials back its loudness. The element of contrast requires that the group size and volume level change to accommodate the conditions that some instruments need in order to be heard clearly.

I have been attending community drum circles of various types for over 25 years. I have been to open events and to workshops led by master drummers. I have heard highly energetic drumming, exquisitely interleaved rhythms, and inspired soloists. Nonetheless, the culture of the drum events I have attended seems to have an unspoken rule that most of the time, everyone plays at once. Dropping out, despite its positive contribution to the contrast in sound level, does not often happen spontaneously. It does happen more often in facilitated drum circles, where the facilitator sculpts subsets of the group by location in the room, by instrument timbre, or by some other attribute of the players or the instruments. In the vocal improvisation settings that I have attended, there has been a great deal more variation in the number of singers active at any given time. These groups do not tend to remain at high-volume, high-energy output for extended periods of time. Neither do most of the instrumental improvisation groups I have attended. They seem to enjoy the variation in expression that come from modulating volume levels from whisper to whirlwind.

The advantage of "all play, all the time" in drum circles is that players get a lot of playing time. Assuming they are actively listening when they are playing and not on autopilot, they gain valuable experience making artistic musical choices in what they play. The disadvantage of "all play, all the time" is that the expressive qualities of low volume levels and small group interactions do not get much opportunity to be heard or experienced. The intimacy of playing in a trio, with constant conversational exchanges among the players, is not possible in a group of 25 or more instrumentalists, whether they be percussionists or pianists.

If you were facilitating a drum circle event, and you wanted to emphasize the musical advantages of not playing all the time, how could you go about it?

The goal is to have the group experience the unique and interactive aspects of music making that can more readily occur in small groups. These include the imitation, conversation, and edgy creativity that goes along with not having an ocean of sound as support. Among the pathways to getting the group to pare down its numbers are sculpting, initiating a "wave" or moving quartet, and actually moving four chairs to the center to create a "fishbowl" group that serves as a model of interaction for the larger group.

Sculpting interesting quartets

During facilitated drum circles, it is common to have the leader showcase smaller ensembles and special combinations of players by telling them to keep going and giving a stop cut cue to the rest of the group. Another approach to sculpting would be to indicate that every group of four adjacent people should cluster together to form a set of playing partners, dividing a group of 40 people into 10 quartets. Some of these, based on attendance, might need to be trios or quintets. You could then alternate between having the whole group play and showcasing each separate quartet in any sequence you choose.

The most natural thing is for children to explore sound by being simple and daring.

It is also simple for adults - a voice and a drum are welcome members of an improvising ensemble.

Part Eight -
Tried and True Sequences from Mary Knysh and Jim Oshinsky

In this section we reproduce some of the ways we have presented improvisation activities using flow in a variety of teaching settings, from formal concerts and adult education to school-based music classes. The activities cover a full spectrum of developmental levels, starting with preschool and progressing up to older players. The authorship of each segment is noted as (MK) or (JO).

For early childhood (pre K-1):
  Breath to Boom (MK)
  Balloon Breath (MK)
  Babble Freeze (MK)
  Heartbeat (MK)
  Hello Song (MK)

For intermediate/middle school:
  Me and We (MK)
  One Quality Groove (MK)
  Rhythm Sticks (MK)
  Musical Home (MK)
  One Sound Around with Boomwhackers (MK)
  Groove 101 (MK)
  Growing the Groove (MK)
  One Minute One Sound Symphony (MK)
  One Sound Circuit (MK)
  One Sound Around (MK)
  Ostinato Story Duets (MK)
  Moving Duet (MK)
  Free Play Quartets (MK)

For adolescents and adults:
  Me and We (MK)
  One Quality Groove (MK)
  Stately Dance (MK)
  Watching Teachers Return to Child (JO)
  Celebration Concert with David Darling (JO)

Some of the above activities by Mary Knysh appeared previously in the volume, *Drum Circles for Specific Population Groups*, edited by Simon Faulkner, © 2021, and in *1,2, Let's All Play* by Mary Knysh and Lulu Leathley, © 2015. The essays by James Oshirsky previously appeared in *Return to Child*, © 2015.

Activities for younger students :

Creating Brain-Based Activity Sequences for Young Children (MK)

When creating a session design for young children it is very important to consider the sequence of activities, how they flow from one activity to another, and the opening and closing rituals. The brain seeks familiarity to enter safely into an activity, therefore providing young learners with predictable, accessible, and fun opening activities will ensure that group is engaged from the very beginning of your session. It is most beneficial to share opening activities that eventually can be led by the children themselves, providing them with leadership experiences during each session.

Once the session has begun in a predictable manner, the brain seeks novelty or new experiences and ideas to keep the level of engagement high. It is beneficial to have open-ended activities where children's creative ideas, movements, and rhythms can continually fuel fresh new variations of familiar songs, games and movement sequences. This balance between the familiar and the novel is essential in shaping a best practice activity sequence for young children.

Breath to Boom (MK)

The younger the age group you are working with, the more important the "attention call" aspect of the activity will be. Bringing the group to focus on a single, controllable aspect of music-making is a necessary first step. In the example below, we use a word that reinforces the focusing.

Jump version
We have all seen rock concerts where the lead singer dramatically jumps up at the end of a song and the band comes to a coordinated stop just when the singer's feet hit the ground. That is the essence of the first Breath to Boom activity. The group breathes together, prepares together, jumps together, and says "Boom" together when their feet land together on the floor. The unity of the actions is mirrored in the unity of the sound, which will also inform the group if they are not completely in sync. We tell the students, "Prepare," and what we mean is twofold - one aspect is mental; focus your attention and get ready to go on a signal. The other aspect is physical; the students take a deep breath, all at the same time, which is the first action in this chain: breathe, prepare, jump, say Boom! The Grammy-winning saxophonist Paul Winter used to call breathing together a "conspiracy," which is its literal meaning.

The Breath to Boom activity begins with the word "prepare" which guides children toward self-awareness in their bodies and mental organizational skills. The goal of this activity is for the group to land on their legs at the same time saying "Boom" together. Self-discipline and self-management are necessary for students to find a group sound together and this seemingly simple challenge can quickly build skills for setting a group goal and achieving it.

If jumping is too stimulating for your group, try the seated and more sedate version in which it is hands that hit the floor rather than feet: The leader and the group are seated on the floor. First, place your hands out in front of you on the floor and invite students to join you as you say the word, "prepare." Next, bring your hands all the way up in the air in front of your body. Stretch your arms up high ("catch a star") and wiggle your fingers up in the air. Request that the group copy your movements.

Emphasize the breath. "Breathe upward through body and out the top of the head (Imagine pulling in chocolate milk from the floor up through your spine and out through the very top of your head)."

Add sound to the movements. From the top notes of your voice (the highest pitch) make a vowel sound (it does not matter which vowel) and slowly siren the notes down as your hands fall to the floor, saying "boom" loudly when you reach the floor. Have the students copy the sound and movement together ("bring the star to the floor"). The students will likely do this at varying times.

Repeat the sound and movement, going from high to low. But this time, invite the students to look around the room and see if they can reach the ground and say "boom" at exactly the same time. Note their progress towards unity and coordination. Try variations on how fast the sounds and movements go.

Repeat a third time. It is usually the third time around that the group is able to land on the floor simultaneously.

Balloon Breath (MK)

This exercise in group breathing, toning, and stretching helps relax the body and center the students' attention.

The leader and the group are seated in a circle on the floor. As preparation, reach into the center and grab some imaginary glue, reminding students that it is *strong and sticky*. Pantomime putting this glue on your bottom so you will be stuck to the floor. This helps the students remain seated on the floor when they stretch forward during this activity. Place both hands on the floor in front of you and say, "what color is our first balloon?" Students will offer color ideas from which you choose one color.

Have everyone put their palms together, fingers facing upwards, in front of their chest.

Say, "Imagine your body is a (any selected color) balloon - take a breath and fill this balloon with as much air as you can." With your hands, show how the balloon grows. Separate your hands as the balloon fills with air until you end up with your hands very wide apart.

Next, blow the air out slowly and slowly slide your upper body forward while your bottom stays on the floor. Your hands will slide forward on the floor in front of your body. Have the group copy you.

The idea is to slide forward as far as possible while keeping your bottom glued to the floor. Stay in this relaxed pose and sing the balloon color. Whatever the color, extend the vowel sounds for as long as possible (1 – 2 minutes). For example, "Bluuuuuuuuuuue." You will need to keep breathing and renewing the sound to keep it going that long. As the body returns to an upright seated position, slide the notes of the vowel higher and higher. Repeat two more times, perhaps with new suggestions for what color the balloon is. This activity builds vocal control to hold a steady pitch, and community/group awareness to get to a unison pitch together. In the repetitions of the activity, the students get practice in naming a variety of colors, while also reaping the benefits of vocal toning for relaxation and mental focus.

Babble/Freeze (MK)

This activity follows Breath to Boom and builds upon its pattern of movements. We begin with the word "Prepare," with the hands placed on the floor, ready to move upwards.

Start in a circle with everyone sitting cross-legged on the floor or seated in chairs.

In this sequence, students begin with their hands on the floor positioned even with the middle of the body. Together, the leader and students say the word "Prepare," "Ready," or the fun Italian version "Pronto" (which means "ready" and interestingly is the way many Italians answer the telephone). This time, when we lift our hands we stop in front of the chest, rather than going up over our heads as we did in Breath to Boom.

For the initial round, the leader models that when the word "Go" is heard students silently wiggle their fingers and hands as fast as possible, and stop when they hear the "1, 2, 3, 4, Freeze!" call. The students freeze in place and hold their hand and finger shapes upon hearing the word "Freeze." To support early childhood curriculum, you can ask students to identify where their hands are frozen; low, middle, high, or somewhere in between. This develops spatial awareness and spatial vocabulary.

In the second round, we add vocal sounds that mimic the finger and hand movements. The leader models finger movements with sounds and says, "This is how my fingers sound. When I say Go, let's see what your fingers have to say." When the leader says, "Go," everyone wiggles their fingers and accompanies the movements with vocal babbling sounds. To stop, the leader counts, "1, 2, 3, 4, Freeze!" Some students may not hear the count if the sound and movement in the room is loud or chaotic, so the leader can use a visual cue instead, asking the students to watch closely for the leader to Freeze – "I Freeze, we all Freeze." To encourage high energy participation, encourage the students to be slightly out of control, using the words, "as fast as possible" often during this activity.

For the third round, the leader once again models wiggling their fingers as fast as possible, matching the movement with a babbling vocal sound. This time, the pitch of the babbling shifts with the position of the hands. When the fingers go up high, it signals everyone to babble with higher pitch. When the fingers go low, it signals a lower pitch. Students are now adding pitch to the free babbling voice and movement. Invite the students to take their own journey in movement to see where their fingers want to go. The leader counts, "1, 2, 3, 4, Freeze!" to stop. Try leading the freeze with no vocal count and use a visual cue instead. Dramatically stop in a frozen shape that is exaggerated and visible for the students to see. Which cue is easier to follow, visual or auditory?

As an extension to this activity, invite students to offer ideas for what shapes they could freeze into, such as: animals, facial expressions, emotional postures, etc.

Heartbeat (MK)

This is a simple cross-the-midline activity that can reveal much about the cognitive development of students. It can be an excellent developmental indicator for teachers as they observe which students find this easy and which struggle.

Begin by asking students to put their two hands on their chest. To combine the sensory input, have them both Listen and Feel "the drum that lives inside their bodies." By asking students this question, you are empowering them to discover for themselves that the heart is like a drum beating inside the body. Next, show the students how to tap their hands over their heart at a steady pulse, while saying the words: "Heart, Beat, Heart, Beat." Model this using both hands at once, and also using a left-right, left-right pattern, one hand after the other. This will lead into "walking hands drumming" when they begin to play the same rhythm pattern on the drums.

After tapping over the heart, move the body percussion rhythm to the legs. Once again, alternate both hands on the legs, saying: "Legs, Legs, Legs, Legs." Stop the group with a "freeze," a count down, or a fade out. Then give them a new pattern to say and play together. For example, the leader plays on their legs first and then crosses their hands into an X shape. As a curriculum connector, the leader can ask the students what letter this looks like. When responding, the students say "X," and now the pattern is spoken as "Legs, X, Legs, X."

Developing a solid sense of a steady beat is a fundamental skill that will support children in all areas of learning, including their ability to track words across a page as they maintain a silent internal rhythm for the words, based on spoken language patterns.

Build upon this activity by inviting children to create many different body drumming variations such as: "legs, legs, head, head" or "feet, feet, legs, legs." The more time children spend experiencing steady beat patterning, the better prepared their brains will be for learning.

Heartbeat/Hello Song (MK)   Audio link: https://bit.ly/hellosongMK

I wrote this song many years ago while working in inner-city early childhood centers. It is great for children to hear such a variety of ways that people around the world greet one another. This song has now become one of my opening rituals and is always a favorite for both the students and me.

In practice, students echo each phrase of the song. I like to vary the way that I sing each greeting so that children can explore a wide range of vocal possibilities. We try singing high, singing low, using a funny voice, an opera voice, a whisper, or acting out any idea that you or they may dream up.

The lyrics of the song are:
Hello, hello. Buenos dias. Bon jour. Guten tag.
Hello, hello. Konichiwa. Selema pagee. Ciao, ciao.

Around the world each and every day we greet each other, smile and say… …"

We introduce the accents, language sounds, and the formal names of various languages from around the world.
Hello hello…that is English - Buenos dias…that is Spanish
Bonjour…that is French - Guten tag…that is German
Hello Hello…that is English - Konichiwa…that's Japanese
Selama pagee.. is Indonesian - Ciao ciao...that's Italian
Hello song with Body Percussion (MK)

In this activity, we combine a ritual session-opening song with body percussion and patterning. This engages the verbal processing areas for the words and cultural information, and the motor areas for the rhythmic elements.

First, have the students sit "crisscross applesauce" on the floor and play the rhythms on their legs using both hands. I usually say a rhythm pattern for the legs out loud. On the syllable "Pat" we tap down on the legs. On the syllable "Cross" the hands cross over one another and play on the opposite leg. This is an excellent" crossing-the-midline" activity. Children enjoy offering their own ideas for varying these body percussion patterns and have come up with some wonderful ideas of their own over the years.

Always invite children to come up with ideas and patterns of their own! The body makes a most delightful drum. Encourage the students to "say what you play" every time. This is not only a powerful rhythmic tool, but it is also a great way for young children to discover new places to drum on their bodies.

While students are tracking each simple body percussion pattern, the leader sings the "Hello-Hello" song and the students echo each phrase in the song. In the middle of the song, the leader invites the students to explore other places on their body that can be played like a drum (e.g.- head, shoulders, belly, heart, legs, floor, shoes, etc.). When the song is sung the second time, change the body percussion pattern to: "Legs, X, Clap It Up." (1,2,3 and 4, which is the same cadence as the rhythm starter: "1,2, Let's all play").

Invite students to add to the pattern: "What shall we add?" "Head?" "How many times?" (It is a good idea to suggest four times or less, because any more than that and the patterns can get quite complex). It is always fun to see how fast students can say and play the patterns, and how slowly they can say and play them as well. This develops self-regulation.

If you have students from other cultures in your group, add their greetings to this song. The song can become a reflection of your classroom community.

"Me and We," a teaching sequence for adolescents and adults beginning with One Quality Sound (MK):

This teaching sequence would typically occur in the middle of a day-long workshop, after the basic group improvisation techniques (solo/ostinato, solo/drone, and free improvisation) have been presented. As preparation for this segment, I set up the room into quartets which will play for two or three minutes each, in sequence. I designate a "road map" for the ensembles; that is, I give them a number in playing order and have them remember which group they receive the music from and which group they send the music to. However, the participants usually arrange themselves into the quartet groups, so the instrument combinations are unpredictable.

To get the group playing, and to hear the ways each group plays together, I might give each ensemble a choice of an improvisational form to explore: solo/ostinato, solo/drone, or free improvisation. Each group then plays a short improvisational piece. They play one after the other with only a few seconds of silence in between groups. Assuming all of the groups succeed in connecting with each other when they play, I would then introduce additional go-rounds, each based on a different challenge to find each other in the music.

The first round uses the vocal version of the One Quality Sound activity. Each group breathes together, raising their arms on the inhale. On the exhale, each group conducts its members to begin a one quality vocal sound together and the group listens to find a simultaneous ending place. This usually lasts the length of one breath. Groups need to use eye contact and body language to end together smoothly. We follow a set sequence of groups around the room until each ensemble has played.

For the next round, we repeat the One Quality Sound activity using instruments, for the length of one breath. Since everyone's arms may not be available to physically cue exactly when to begin, we use a head nod or another common body gesture to begin together, and a similar gesture to cooperatively reach a common ending.

In One Quality Sound, the goal of each player is to maintain the uniqueness of their own sound without adjusting or "sweetening" the sound to adjust to the sounds of their peers. The activity emphasizes that the "we" is composed of several "me's," each with a distinct identity, making a combination with its own quality, be it consonant or full of tension.

One Quality Groove – moving from "Me" to "We" (MK)

As a way of highlighting a contrasting playing principle, the next activity involves players entering not with a single held note, but with a specific repeating groove of their own. The activity asks them to discover one group groove that they all agree upon as quickly as possible. When the groove is discovered and all players are playing exactly the same rhythmic groove, they quickly stop. The idea is to move quickly from "me" to "we," sharing individual ideas and flexibly giving way to the ideas of others, collaborating to find a common groove as quickly as possible. This requires players to surrender any rigid attachment they may have to their own contribution for the sake of the group.

In the last round, the groups play in ensembles around the room using any of the improvisation forms from the session.

For a verbal reflection on the group process, at the end each quartet takes a few minutes to share what worked well in their ensemble and what they might change or enhance for next time. When they put their learning in words, it gives them a chance to reflect on, consolidate, and keep what has been taught.

Rhythm Games Using Sticks (MK):

Playing percussion patterns with partners using sticks is a very portable and accessible way of working with cooperation and collaboration in a musical format. Although the activity can unfold in many sequences, here is one that has proven useful in workshops with people from age 8-adult.

To begin, the leader invites participants to step in time and join a steady beat with their feet in a relaxed way. Depending on the age level and maturity level of the group, the leader next introduces two sounds in an African drum language: On the sound Goon, the players strike their own sticks together. On the sound Pah, the sticks are played silently in the air. With younger groups, the players only pick up their sticks after the sounds have been taught.

Next, the leader gives simple Goon/ Pah rhythmic calls for the participants to echo back vocally and to echo using their sticks. Once the format of call and response can be reliably followed by the group, the leader invites each person in the circle to make up a simple call/echo pattern, say it aloud, and play it to the group. The group echoes the pattern and leadership moves to the next person. This proceeds until everyone has had a chance to create a pattern and have their pattern echoed back to them by the group. This part of the activity demonstrates equal belonging and welcoming, and gives each person a small, controlled experience of being in the leadership role.

For the next phase of the activity, the group is divided into pairs. First, the leader invites a participant to assist in modeling the partner creative process. The leader and partner make up a simple goon-pah spoken pattern, agree upon it, and decide how to play this pattern using the sticks. This time, on the sound Goon the participants hit their own sticks together. On the sound Pah the partners hit their sticks together in any way they think would work. The leader can offer a variety of ideas, giving permission for people to improvise and create many Pah variations – playing high in the air, low down, behind the back, one side then the other, etc.

When all of the participants have found a partner, each pair creates a Goon/Pah sticking pattern. They are coached to say and play the pattern as they create and practice, which is an example of sing what you play. The pairs get about three minutes to create their patterns. Next, each pair shares their patterns with group. This is a very important part of the process. The pairs share their pattern by saying and playing it at the same time. To emphasize the balance between individuality and diversity, the leader can ask the group to look for similarities and unique differences in each pattern.

As extensions of the basic pair activity, the leader can invite a group of two people to find another pair and create a group of four. The quartet will create a new Goon/Pah pattern together. They can repeat the stick activity, or to introduce the element of pitch, each person can have the option of trading a stick for a Boomwhacker, a pitched plastic tube. After developing a new pattern for about three minutes, each group of four gets to share their pattern with the group. If a quartet forgets their pattern, or stumbles in any way, be sure to give them more time to organize themselves before putting them in the position of sharing their pattern with the group. The primary goal in this activity is a feeling of success. Lastly, the leader can remind the group to look for similarities, differences, and unique qualities in the patterns.

At the next level of complexity, the activity can be set to a steady pulse and the patterns combined into a group composition. First, the leader offers a steady beat on a drum while the groups listen to the beat and use the beat as the bass rhythm for their patterns. The leader provides all the groups with time to practice playing their Goon/Pah pattern over the drum pulse and make any necessary rhythmic adjustments. The leader reminds players to practice looping their patterns so they can end and immediately begin again.

The leader constructs a group composition by building the parts, one layer at a time. The groups are invited to add their pattern to the overall sound, one by one, while the drumbeat continues playing. Although the music make become dense or complex, each group keeps their own pattern going when the other groups enter in. The leader points out the features of the group composition, the collaborative result of all patterns played over the steady beat. It is always exciting for players to see how their patterns can work together over a single heartbeat rhythm. Once all groups have joined the composition, the leader may invite each group (one by one) to stop playing and listen to the collective composition without their pattern and then rejoin to notice how their composition enhances the overall musical piece.

To model how the group can adapt to changing situations and challenges, the leader can speed up and slow down the steady beat. The groups need to adjust their patterns and work together to keep their patterns coordinated. If time allows, this is a wonderful time in the process to invite participants to continue to "play what they sing." Each person says their group patterns aloud and walks over to another available drum or percussion instrument in the room, transferring their pattern from voice to drum. The group now hears their collaborative composition played in a new way on these new instruments.

At the very end, the leader provides the group with some time to reflect upon the creative process:
How did it feel to create alone?
What was the difference when you worked in teams of two?
What did you notice when the group grew to four?
What did you learn about yourself and the others in your group during this process?
What was your favorite part of the activity? What part was challenging for you?

Musical Home – a Collaboration for school-age classes and large groups (MK)

More than a rhythm pattern, the "musical home" is a short, repeatable rhythmic composition that includes timbre, articulation, and dynamics. Created and owned by the class through collaborative music-making, the musical home is notated, shared, and given a place of honor in the classroom. It is a musical family portrait, and each member of the family is represented.

The musical home is a safe and secure musical idea. With it, we can: come to attention, share our feelings, grow together, remember what collaboration looks and feels like, embrace and celebrate our communal identity, and explore new ways of thinking with a safe place to return.

The process involves an organic gathering and funneling process that repeats at the level of the individual and at the level of the group. The pattern: cast a wide net of broad ideas, then winnow them down to essential elements and "keepers." The selecting of ideas in the end is a collective decision. The emergent wisdom of the group is a terrific model of giving up one's own ideas to serve and support the greater community.

The activity begins with an exploration phase focused on the individual (Me). This is a time of expansion and brainstorming where the group seeks novelty and new ideas to spark engagement and growth. Depending on the available equipment, we first invite students to play freely on their instruments – to "go on a little *sound vacation*," and try out as many new ideas as possible. We encourage open exploration without judging. To open up the territory of texture, timbre, and volume, we ask - How many different ways can we find to make sound?

The next stage is a contraction phase in which we simplify and clarify the ideas that were generated in exploring, and we use this more refined set of ideas to compose. We ask each person to choose two sounds and create a repeating pattern (ostinato) that represents you. Having explored many sound possibilities, they have many ideas to choose from as they create. The group plays their individually chosen pieces together at once.

After each person chooses a two-sound "signature" pattern, we listen and appreciate the resultant group composition. We invite students to notice where their patterns fit in the overall composition, what patterns are similar, and which are different. What contrasts make for interesting combinations when we listen with "big ears."

When we repeat the process at the group level, we return to an exploration phase. This time, the free instrumental play has a broader focus and shifts from your exploration to our exploration (We). Now we notice which ideas are being shared by other students, and we imitate the ideas of others to expand our possibilities and our musical vocabulary. This is followed by a second contraction phase in which we once again simplify, clarify, and compose. The group chooses two sounds again, creating a new ostinato that represents this second journey and exploration. This segment ends when we listen and appreciate the resultant group composition. This time when we invite students to notice the new group composition we ask - Were the patterns more connected and more alike? And - What effect did listening to one another and imitating each other have on the group composition?

The third time through the process, the goal is to arrive at sounds and patterns that reflects the way the group wants to see itself (Ours). The goal of this exploration time is to notice the emergent big idea from the group. The task is for all the players to listen for one idea that everyone can find and play exactly together.

In the third contraction phase, through an organic process of collaboration the group finds unison. They achieve this by saying "yes" to the big idea that begins to emerge from the group. It may be necessary to simplify the idea until all players can play this new rhythmic pattern in unison. Next, the group listens to the home rhythm that has been created by the group and appreciates their composition. To preserve it, we ask - How would you say this pattern? And we explore a variety of vocal sounds that will help everyone remember the pattern. From playing and saying the pattern simultaneously, we shift to voice only and invite the group to listen and agree upon one spoken pattern that represents their home rhythm. Lastly, we explore a variety of ways that this home rhythm could be notated (e.g.- African box notation, standard notation, realization score, and other creative ideas).

One Sound Around Game Sequence

This game provides an excellent example of Listen, Connect, Communicate, and Create. It can be played with any combination of instruments, voice or body percussion, but it is particularly fun and engaging with boomwhackers (pitched plastic tubes). Each player has one boomwhacker and strikes it with a rhythm stick to create the best sound.

The first stage is called "Pass It." The first player plays one sound and then looks to connect eyes with the player on their right. The next player does the same (play then look). This process continues to move many times around the circle until all players can listen to and appreciate the resultant composition they are creating.

The next level of the activity introduces a change of direction. As the sound moves around the circle, any player may now look back at the player that sent them a sound and play two sounds back to them while saying, "turn it." The sound reverses direction and moves in the opposite direction around the circle. The composition will now have an unpredictable spatial component as it moves right and left around the circle. Invite players to listen to the changing composition as the direction changes.

In addition to passing the sound and changing the direction of the sound, the next level of the game introduces the option to toss the sound to a player at another seat in the circle. The most important aspect of the game to pre-teach is how to make a clear connection so the receiver knows the sound is coming to them. Model this with a dramatic body movement and clear eye contact. Now there are three ways the sound can pass – look, turn and toss. Listen for how the sound composition changes with linear movement, direction changes, and skips across the circle.

From single sounds, the game can be expanded to pass short expressive musical phrases.

Creativity and Risk Taking ~ Groove 10

Groove 101 establishes a common pulse, which is the jumping off place for rhythmic coordination and exploration. The three main roles of improvisation – support, solo, and silence are presented in a dynamic and personalized activity, using rhythms that derive from the student's familiar names, places, and previous rhythm activities.

The first stage of the activity establishes a steady pulse. To be felt viscerally and taken into the body, the pulse is best played on deep, low drums or other objects (large bins) that make a low, muffled sound. Recruit a few students to be the Beat Keepers, who will keep this steady pulse going in regular rhythm, like the tic-toc of a clock. To spread the pulse around the classroom so all can hear it and feel it, have at least two Beat Keepers, seated opposite each other if the class is in a circle. Since this role is repetitive and requires both regularity and stamina, allow Beat Keepers to leave this role at any time and find a replacement from among their classmates. It will help to have a rule that if you are invited to be a Beat Keeper you have to accept.

The next stage adds a new layer of rhythm over the steady pulse. It can be a simple repeating rhythm that is drawn from other lessons of the day, from the students' names or the school's name, or from the rhythms that emerged from the previous rhythm activities. What is most important is that the rhythm is simple, memorable, and repeated over and over as an ostinato or loop. Everyone except the Beat Keepers plays this rhythm, which becomes the "home" and provides contrast.

In the third stage of the activity students will have free rein to explore rhythmic improvisation over the grounding rhythms set by the Beat Keepers and the students holding down the "home" rhythm. In "explore for four," the students get four beats to fill in with whatever creative patterns they can come up with, followed by a return to the "home" rhythm. There are potentially three layers of rhythm in this activity, with Beat Keepers, a section repeating the "home" rhythm, and one or more students alternating from free exploring back to the "home" rhythm with four beats on each. Or the whole class (other than the Beat Keepers) can alternate between the "home" rhythm and individual exploring. If the students can manage individual exposure, the exploring can be done one student at a time.

As an alternative to having four beats of exploration, the group can hold the beat in inner hearing during four beats of silence, then return to the "home" rhythm. Once they have experienced "home," exploring, and silence, they can make up their own patterns using these three building blocks.

Growing the Groove

A solid and infectious rhythm inspires development. The first step in establishing a groove is to set up the basis for rhythmic entrainment. This is a steady pulse in regular rhythm.

The next layer is a repeating "home" rhythm that is based on a familiar phrase, or a person's name. To find additional rhythms that work well with the "home" rhythm, the class explores freely and discovers emergent new rhythms that are interlocking in interesting ways.

Once the class is playing the "home" rhythm in a solid and coordinated way together, it may be possible to drop the pulse. When the group has entrained together, the pulse is kept in the body and inner hearing, without having to be played. It is expected that students will sometimes lose their way during their rhythmic explorations. The advantage of having a "home" rhythm is that there is always a safe and predictable playing pattern to return to and rejoin the group.

The group pattern can become more intricate if the group can hold onto the basic pulse and the "home" rhythm on their own. The periods of exploration can become longer, from 4 beats to 8 beats or more. In place of a "home" rhythm and free exploration, you can introduce periods of silence, followed by a dramatic return to the groove. If the players can manage the exposure, individuals can solo for 4 or 8 beats. This can be done with three different background sounds – the pulse, the "home" rhythm, or silence.

The activity begins with an organizing structure that is external – there is a pulse given by the leader and kept up by the "Beat Keepers." The next layer, the "home" rhythm, is solicited from the class, then played in unison by the group. The third stage adds short periods of exploration over the regular beat. Depending on the group's ability to keep the structure going, you can have more explorers at once or fewer. If the group can sustain the community groove, they can be permitted to truly "make it their own" through freedom to create more interesting variations. This groove can become an organic collaboration that grows and changes when everyone contributes to its life with their active listening. A dramatic element of silence allows the development of inner hearing and cements the group rhythm when everyone resumes playing together in unison.

One Sound One Minute Symphony

The goal of this simple structure is to create a group composition in a very short time. Starting with silence, each player adds one repeating sound to the symphony. As the sounds combine, the players are encouraged to listen to the composition as it emerges. Notice what sounds stand alone and what sounds are splashed over one another. The students will have to listen carefully to find the natural ending.

One Sound Circuit

The goal of this game is to create a sound circuit around the circle and to build skills for connection, communication, and speed. This game can be played with voice, body percussion, and all instruments. This is a boom-whacker favorite!

The first player plays one sound and then looks to connect eyes with the player on their right. The next player does the same (Play then Look). This passes around the entire circle. When it returns to player one, Stop.

Someone agrees to be the timer and times the circuit cycle. The group runs the circuit three or four times to arrive at their best and most efficient time.

Ostinato/Story Duets

Up to now, each player made one sound and stopped playing when the sound was passed. In the next variation, each player plays a short expressive phrase and then changes it to a short repeating pattern (ostinato). They repeat this pattern over and over without stopping. Instead of passing the short expressive phrase and dropping out, the first player changes their short expressive phrase into a simple repeating pattern. This becomes a support rhythm for another player's sound story. The second player explores various sounds and settles in on an extended short expressive phrase, over the pattern provided by the first player. It is important to keep eye contact between the two players during the duet.

A Moving Duet

When the player is finished with their sound story and has settled into a repeating pattern, they shift their gaze to another player on the circle, inviting a third player to solo over their support rhythm. Player one stops as soon as player two looks elsewhere and locks gaze with a new partner. As the game progresses, it is helpful to remind those that have played to place their hands on their laps so that it is clear who has not played yet. Players that have not gone yet can also be reminded to look at the player who is seeking a new partner to let them know they would like to play.

Free Play Quartets

Once all players have had the opportunity to play in a duet, this game can move into a quartet form by having the last two duet players each invite one new player to the game. The duet players and their two new players all engage in a free play quartet. The focus of these small groups is listening, imitation, and communication as they create a spontaneous composition together. After a few minutes, the four quartet players are asked to pass their part to a new player with a visual cue. When the new player begins, the player that invited them to join stops playing. As new players enter these evolving quartets, they need to look around and identify the other members of this new quartet that has been formed. At any point during the game, quartet players can pass their part off to a new player with a visual cue. This is a wonderful way to keep all players in the room engaged and attentive in the music making process.

Stately Dance activity, adapted for a large group (MK)

At one MfP workshop, each of us on staff was asked to model a Music for People skill or concept in both whole-group format and as a small ensemble experience. The idea was to create seamless shifts from one format to the other, using a minimum of words.

There are many MfP structures that work incredibly well with all improvisors, regardless of their prior musical experiences. But some instrument groups present specific challenges. One struggle I have had is with those who play guitar and piano, as they tend to improvise in a manner that locks the ensemble into a repeating pattern of chord changes. I try to encourage them to discover a much more open-ended approach so they can vary their contribution and interaction in an ensemble.

The Stately Dance activity has always been a form that I love, due to its simplicity and elegance. Each player offers one single note in a common rhythm and this becomes a support system to solo over. It is the simplicity and the "feel" of the dance that makes it completely unthreatening to enter this structure; yet the combination of notes serves to build a rather sophisticated chord or cluster for a soloist to play over. The first time around, the chord builds as each player enters. Then, on the second go-round, each player changes their note, creating constantly shifting tonalities. The third time around, the chord or cluster changes after each player solos, ending on a new note. Simplicity and complexity both abound in this form.

One of the reasons I chose this form to share was because it begins in the body and voice. I invited everyone to stand and step to this rhythm: short, long – short, long. I asked them to imagine themselves dancing in a Medieval castle in a very regal and graceful manner. There is such beauty to this rhythm, and such simplicity.

From here I invited everyone to sing one note as they moved, keeping to the same short-long rhythm. While dancing and singing this rhythm around the room, they were able to interact with others and hear their notes, taking into their bodies both the rhythms and the resulting layers of intervals happening around the room.

I then asked everyone in the group to change their note on the count of four, all at the same time, while continuing the stepped dance and movement. Immediately the room was alive with an entirely different chord/cluster. From here as they stepped, I asked them to change their note when they met someone with a note that appealed to them. This meant the group chord was beginning to change in a much more random and free style.

The players walked back over to their chairs and their instruments, and I invited everyone to find the same note they were vocalizing using their instruments. In this way they transferred to a seated version of the dance, using their instruments. This supported the skill of "sing what you play, play what you sing."

I invited the group to find a final note together to close this community composition and then we moved to the ensemble version of the Stately Dance form. I was still holding in mind that I wanted the entire group to experience the ensemble form of this structure, so I did not break the mood or the momentum by describing the game in verbal detail.

The room was already set up in ensembles (with chairs arranged in quartets), so I set up an all-group experience in this way: I mentally divided the group into four sections. I chose one person to be the leader of each section, which was a combination of two or three quartets. In all, I set up four group leaders and four groups of followers.

Each group leader was cued to begin playing the short-long Stately Dance rhythm using one note on their instrument. The followers sang their section leader's note in unison, thus keeping the entire group involved and engaged with the structure. In MfP language, the players shadowed their leader.

For the first round of this version of Stately Dance, one at time, each leader added their note to the rhythm and each group sang that note along with their leader. On the second time around, one at a time each group leader changed their note and the group sang the new note, carefully matching the texture and timbre of these notes and listening to keep their sound less loud than the leader's note. The third time around the leaders each soloed over the layers created by the combination of the leaders' four instruments and their four groups' vocals.

At the end I invited the whole group to sustain their final notes, so the entire ensemble ended with a lovely final sustained vocal chord.

Since the group was already seated in quartets, it was a simple transition from this all-group experience to invite each quartet around the room to experience the Stately Dance form one by one and see how the large group activity informed and inspired the individual ensembles.

Alison Weiner, Mary Knysh, Ange Chianese, Jim Oshinsky and others enjoy a ukelele jam.

A possible Social Music Improvisation workshop format for school teachers:

Teachers Return to Child (JO)

Where does music begin? When children are young and not self-conscious, they interact in the world through play and experimentation.   Music activates and mobilizes children to dance, to imitate sounds, and to be curious about how the sounds are made. Children naturally are moved by the interesting sounds they hear - they listen actively, with body involvement (and they do not readily sit still). When this natural interest in music is encouraged, the music that children hear provides the basis for how they become able to play with music independently, holding melodies and rhythms in their imaginations, and creating new tunes and songs that express their moods. This impulse to make music is innate in all of us - how do any of us ever lose it?

Some years ago, I taught a two-week summer class for public school teachers on "Music Improvisation in the Classroom." The 15-hour course attracted a mixed group of general education and music teachers from elementary through high school. The content was based on the "inside-out" approach to music-making, as taught by the organization Music for People, with links to traditional curriculum areas in math (patterning), literature (soundtracks), and social studies (culture, styles, instrument groups). The nature of the class also emphasized some of the social benefits of arts instruction in general, and of working in cooperative groups in particular.

By "inside-out," I mean the musical ideas come from the students themselves, as expressions of their energy, their emotions, and their desire to make connections with each other through their sounds in small groups and ensembles. In contrast, an "outside-in" approach would have students mainly imitate music that was composed by others or have them learn to read music notes before playing by ear. Some well-established music education systems also employ aspects of an "inside-out" approach. In the Suzuki system of instrumental music training, the ear/hand connection is taught for years through listening activities before note-reading is introduced. (See the Suzuki website for further information about the Suzuki method of instrumental instruction).

The course was set up so that the first half was entirely experiential. In the second half of the course, the teachers were encouraged to design and try out lesson plans that combined music improvisation with their own teaching areas. They also tried their hand at conducting and facilitating Music for People activities from the Return to Child curriculum.

In the experiential part of the course, music improvisation was introduced through playful whole group activities. Such activities generally provide safety through anonymity. Rhythm games began with a pulse and added layers until complex rhythmic textures were created that provided a ground for soloing. In similar fashion, melody games began with a vocal drone and added harmonies. The rhythms were sometimes introduced on recording, to give the group a strong pulse to follow. Then it was possible to fade down the recorded music level and launch the group into its own improvisational territory. The parallel to this with melody was to start with a held drone in 5ths, and fade that out once the group had tuned in. I used a shruti box (a reed bellows instrument from India) but taping down two notes on a portable keyboard organ would accomplish the same purpose.

The least musically experienced teachers particularly appreciated the atmosphere of acceptance and non-judgment that was established from the first-class activities. As the class progressed, their reaction logs showed that they became less afraid and less inhibited as they realized that the major criticisms they faced were not external but internal. Long-held ideas about being unmusical, unable to hold a beat or disliking one's own voice surfaced and yielded to new self-images based on musical successes within the class.

Teachers realized that the common ways they had been taught music - through choral singing, music appreciation, and instrumental ensembles - did not prepare them for making their own music, using music to express feelings, or socially connecting to others via music. While every teacher had the experience growing up of bringing home some of their own artwork and creative writing, none had ever been encouraged to do anything similar with music. The music teachers among the group confirmed that they had thought of improvisation as the most advanced skill rather than the most basic one. It was clear that the sequence of musical skills taught in this course was the exact opposite of what they were used to. In this course, the beginning spot was the desire to make some form of personal music, as simple as tapping with the beat, or as complex as an extended solo or improvised ensemble. By the end of the class the teachers had all grasped the concept that the desire to make personal and social music was a strong motivation for learning more technique on an instrument or voice. This was true for students and teachers alike.

I have often heard Music for People's cofounder, cellist David Darling, say, "Be a Master of what you can control." In this statement is the key to sensitive musicianship. Even if you are the most inexperienced novice in music, there are still some sounds you do have control over. If you employ even one sound on the basis of sensitive listening and the kind of assertiveness that comes from paying attention to your surroundings, your sounds will be indistinguishable from a virtuoso's. As you gain in musical experience, you master more sounds and become more fluent with them. But mastering the balance of sound and silence, the "When" to play as well as "What" to play, seems to derive from a different category of skills altogether. An ensemble of experienced musicians can wow an audience with technique, but there can be just as much drama in an improvised performance in which the participants are interacting authentically. This exposes the social interactions among the players that happen to take place in sound. When the timing or volume of a group shifts in ways to accommodate the weakest member of the ensemble, when the group makes it work for everyone unselfishly, you can see the power of the improvisation setting to serve as a model for all sorts of other human interactions. As the class progressed, the teachers certainly began to master more sounds. More importantly, they grasped the concept that permission to engage in play-based exploration led to deep and integrated learning. Their comments showed that this humanistic educational philosophy could be applied to curriculum areas outside of music. The central idea is to create a classroom atmosphere where risk is respected, and safety is reasonably assured for all students.

In addition to communicating an overall philosophy of acceptance, one of the goals of the class was to provide teachers with a bag of tricks for introducing improvised music into their classes, while at the same time addressing their fears that spontaneous (and potentially loud) activities would be too chaotic for the tolerance level of their schools. When I taught my children to ride bicycles, the first thing I taught them was how to stop. This took care of some of the fear and made learning to balance and ride somewhat easier. Similarly, I looked to teach the teachers "platform skills" for group facilitation and basic conducting techniques, so they could feel somewhat secure that their own groups would not get out of control. This helped the educators respect the process of learning through natural curiosity and play and limited their need to introduce more predictable and uniform sequences of skills in an effort to maintain order.

The philosophy of the class was to create activities that would be inherently fun to participate in, emphasizing the anonymity of whole-group participation before introducing smaller ensembles. The teachers needed to become familiar and gain some experience in all of the activities they might use in their classrooms, yet they had to be approached as adults rather than artificially role-playing as if they were children. It was more important and valuable for them to make their own music and experience the judgments and inhibitions that arose, as well as the possible approaches a leader could take to melt those judgments.

It was clear in working with these teachers that permission to make sound and music has been all but conditioned out of many adults. All of the teachers reported feeling fearful about improvising and some were pointedly self-critical. I often notice some of the same processes going on in myself when I try to reconcile the shyness I feel about performing with the comfort I feel about teaching sound-making. The key seems to be that when I use sound in a group, whether it is a sigh/tone that is part of long-breath relaxation training, or a brief rhythm drummed on a lap or tapped out on water canisters or flowerpots, I have relatively little judgment about it. In fact, any sounds that come out after judgment is suspended are going to be OK. This is the hidden (or not so hidden) music therapy aspect of Music for People-inspired teaching. The major goal is to establish an atmosphere where hypercritical self-talk is mostly silenced. Then each person has a clear and large enough palette to be instinctively creative. As an improviser you can always repeat what you particularly like, discard what you don't like, and strive to get your body to cooperate with what your mind's ear is hearing. When working with students, one of the leader's first jobs may be to establish ground rules for giving supportive feedback and limiting outside criticism from peers. The group of teachers quickly felt the difference between an atmosphere in which each new step was applauded and one in which the main form of communication was evaluative feedback, whether nice or nasty.

For this summer's group that consisted of mainly adults with no musical training or current skill, I needed to be specific about providing an ample supply of building blocks for improvisations. Much of what I found myself teaching was about contrasts: loud/soft, fast/slow, yea/oooh, silence/sound, chord 1/chord 2, strong accent/weak, busy spots/holes in the sound, etc. Some teachers were able to use rhythmic variation to create interest in a one-note solo. Contrasts identify edges, including personal edges. If someone was already comfortable with mouth percussion, I'd ask them to try a long vocal tone. If someone was only making quiet sounds, I'd ask them to try a loud one.

Here's an example: when the whole group was secure holding a pulse, I cut the group and conducted half of them to double the pulse, then I had the two groups switch parts. I cut the group again and introduced a contrasting pattern, so that three parts were going. When all of the sub-groups had played each part, I invited volunteer soloists to solo over the top (unless I had spontaneous soloists already going). Over this rhythm structure, I cut a small section of the group to hold long tones. Functioning as a "horn section," I led this subgroup in stacking a harmony. (Stacking means building a chord on top of a root note, such as when the 3 Stooges sing "hello, hello, hello" and make a major triad - CEG). We did this with long tones, then with long tones with a staccato ending rhythm. Then we used just the staccato phrase. This illustrated many of the roles they could take in an ensemble improvisation, from pulse-holder to soloist, from making constant sound to emphasizing silence.

Whenever I worked with a smaller group such as a duet or quartet in a fishbowl in the center of the working space, I encouraged the surrounding group to listen actively (or listen-in). I did this by specifically having them either imitate the parts they heard or play a variety of air-instruments. Playing air-drums and shakers helped the whole group strongly hold the pulse of the inner working group. Having the large group participate as soloists with air-instruments helped the more inhibited ones take risks as they experienced the music in their heads with no risk of embarrassment. They were later more willing to move from air-instruments to vocal imitation of their "air" solos.

Another emphasis within the class was on "listening out." This took many forms, from listening to the long sustain of a bell or a held piano key as it faded into the ambient sounds of the room, to harmonizing with the hums of the lighting and machines in the space, to playing all of the available objects in the room, musical instruments or furniture. This led to a homework assignment to bring in household objects that made interesting sounds. When these objects were assembled, I arranged duets between the objects and the actual instruments they most resembled, such as pot lids, drinking cups and metal candle holders with other bells and gongs, a cheese grater with a zydeco washboard, etc. When the teachers created their own quartets of found-instrument ensembles, the high level of listening made for well-connected and coordinated improvisations in their groups.

Some individuals who were less fluent when given an open-ended opportunity to solo did well when they had some parameters within which to solo. If anyone became stuck, a suggestion to make up a melodic phrase that expressed a particular emotion often worked to unstick them. The same was true for suggestions to make up a phrase with some cultural or ethnic connection. Paradoxically, playing the stuck feeling often unstuck the person playing it. This led to the idea that authentic sounds are always useful building blocks for expressive solos and improvisations.

By the midway point in the course, I gave the teachers a checklist / matrix of everything they had done in the first eight hours. When they saw what they had done as improvisers - holding pulses and creating rhythms, functioning in small ensembles as accompanists and soloists, conducting the group to start and stop, go fast and slow, get loud and soft, and giving feedback in a way that supports each person growing more comfortable taking risks - they showed that they owned the content by spontaneously offering more connections between the academic areas they teach and the music activities they were learning.

All of the teachers present, even the full-time music teachers, tended to use a primarily verbal teaching style in the classes they teach during the school year. While students need to pay attention to get the verbal instructions, the type of listening any of us employ to grasp verbal meaning is not the same as the type of listening we would use to tell if we are playing in tune, or if we are playing what is in our mind's ear. In order to maintain active musical listening, it is helpful to give instructions through a separate communication channel, for example, through pantomime and other visual cues. Many of the activities I led used primarily visual signs for instructions, or else the small segments of verbal instructions were worked in while the class was engaged in keeping a beat or doing call-and-response. Anything I asked the participants to do I was willing to model, and the modeling was usually more clear than any verbal instruction might have been. Especially for a group such as this was, inexperienced in improvisation, any verbal explanation I might have given could have been seized on as the "right" way to complete some improvisational activity. This could have limited the options for responding. Sometimes even the best verbal instructions about music miss the boat while models and live examples serve as more specific guideposts. By modeling in place of explaining, I left the activities far more open-ended and accepting of each individual's personal interpretation. The more we "just did it" without extensive verbal preparations, the more willing the group was to dive into activities in general.

By the second half of the course, when the teachers were leading their own lessons, I encouraged them to use a minimum of verbal instructions. Some used none at all and were pleased to see how well the visual channel worked to maintain the group's attention.

We end this presentation of teaching sequences with a description of the way our mentor David Darling organized a concert as a chain of improvised pieces. He used all of the principles we have been writing about, weaving whole group unison activities with selected and sculpted smaller ensembles, introducing contrasting timbres and musical styles, adding drama by featuring soloists and duets, all while maintaining participant and audience interest through a two-hour high-quality musical performance that was entirely improvised in a continuous flow. All of our work reflects his influence and example.

The Celebration - Organic Flow in a Live Improvised Concert (JO)

When was the last time you saw a concert that was 100% improvisation? The typical answer, even amongst followers of jazz, jam-bands, or music from India might be "never." These musical styles each incorporate improvisation into their standard formats, with instrumentalists playing over predictable chord changes or rhythm patterns. The players occasionally go further "out there" into free-form exploration, and they often return to a recognizable structure.

This evening is different. 100% improvisation, unscripted. Two hours of organic flow, with influences from classical to blues, incorporating a chorus, a percussion ensemble, and both professional and amateur players on standard and folk instruments. You can be there in the audience. The more unusual fact is that you can also be there on stage.

The scene is the acoustically pristine Rausch concert hall at the State University of New York at Fredonia. A week-long workshop on music improvisation is drawing to a close, and for its culminating event, the whole group of participants, nearly 70 in all, are about to be led through an evening of improvisation by cellist David Darling.

The concert begins in silence. Darling takes a position as a conductor at the center of the ensemble, which forms a large semicircle across the width of the stage. He has the whole group begin vocally, imitating the sound of a shaker in rhythm. He gestures to indicate some parts of the group to continue, and others to stop playing. The sounds develop a sense of space - left, right, center.

He builds energy, then stops the group and indicates a female vocalist in the choir loft above the stage level. She begins a spontaneous solo - high and plaintive, soaring and resonating. While she is singing, Darling is indicating four players to take seats at center stage, like a chamber music quartet. A violin, a viola, an avant-garde vocalist, and a jazz guitar. When the vocalist in the balcony finishes, the quartet begins. The style is not quite namable - modern classical sounds, angular and percussive, but with vocalizing, mirrored by a combination of male and female voices. The players are clearly listening to each other, imitating each other, harmonizing, answering, and most of all, leaving space for new things to develop.

Flash back to earlier in the workshop week. A mixed group of musicians has been divided into pairs. Each pair stands face to face, with hands raised and touching. Their eyes are closed. The leader asks one member of each pair to initiate movement, and the other member to follow as sensitively as they can. The roles then reverse, with the leader becoming the follower. The next variation has the two members giving up the idea of leading and following, and just moving in a coordinated manner, connected by their hands. Then the same concepts are applied to musical duets, beginning with one partner mirroring the other in sound, then reversing roles, and ending with connected improvisation beyond leading and following. After a week of activities such as this, the group is primed for improvised duets, trios, and quartets.

Keeping a step or two ahead, Darling has indicated a certain player to take the seat at the grand piano. When the quartet ends, the whole group sings, matching the quartet's last note in unison. Everyone plays with tension and release by singing a half step above the unison, bending into one crisp tone, then sliding a half step below. The group stacks harmonies and articulates short sharp rhythms with precision. When the singing stops, the pianist begins a deep and complex exploration. Her playing has the immediacy of creation and the detail of a composition. We are witness to a soundtrack for which there is no film. Her playing moves the group, but when she is done, their appreciation is shown by the way they allow the silence to linger, adding to the weight of the music that preceded it.

In the meantime, Darling has arranged another quartet of all female voices, consisting of women from 14 to over 40. By ear alone, you cannot tell which are the younger and which are the older voices. They blend, they weave, and they pull back to leave room for solos. As conductor, Darling is relentlessly positive in his directing. The most common word he utters is "Yes!" In fact, the concert has no announcements, and no breaks in its flow from any explanations or set-ups. Sounds arise, ensembles blend and morph into new structures, and occasionally there are powerful silences. It is a listener's dream come true.

The evening continues and includes segments in a few recognizable musical styles. A bass player walks a jazz line, and an electric guitar joins in, followed by a trumpet and subtle hand percussion. A classical guitarist plays nylon strings in the style of a Bach etude, but not one that was ever written. He is joined by a woodwind, and their group is followed by a digeridoo. A violin solos over the drone of the aboriginal horn, and the group is surrounded by a dozen people tilting rain sticks, washing the players in lateral waves. None of these ensembles were pre-chosen. Each was indicated by the conductor within seconds of beginning to play. This is a concert an expert is weaving from the materials in front of him - whole group, solos, small groups, silence.

Two hours go by. No intermission. The energy rises for hot coordinated drumming on djembes and dumbecs, and the energy mellows for gongs and glass bowls. The players know that at any moment they may be called on to play in some combination they have never experienced before, and they are ready. The music is at times highly personal and emotional, and if there are tears, they flow. Throughout it all, the music is about listening. The silences are pervasive and intentional. One note, one quality sound can be enough for a sonic meal.

How do you get 70 people, most of whom had no knowledge of each other only a week before, to play this broad a program of music? That is the unique skill of David Darling, Mary Knysh, Julie Weber, Lynn Miller, David Rudge, Irene Feher, Ron Kravitz, and other teachers of a methodology called Music for People. It involves a particular nontraditional definition of musicality, beginning with listening skills, and building mastery of articulation and expression through the medium of solo and ensemble improvisation. The techniques are taught with commitment to a humanistic mindset - that all people are musical, and that there are no wrong notes. Develop a compassionate and accepting ear, and you can encourage your own rapid musical growth, allowing for learning through experience. In this atmosphere of support, anyone can join the community of musicians, and succeed by sharing their own music.

Breanna Metcalf-Oshinsky leads a group vocal activity at a Music for People event.

David Darling sits in with an all-cello quartet.

Part Nine -
Social Music Improvisation Activities for Band, Orchestra, and Chorus

Let improvising be a regular and normalized element of how your ensembles warm up. Start with tuning – many orchestras and bands begin with an oboe (or other wind or string) who gives a concert A for the group to use for tuning purposes. Sometimes the section leaders give reference notes to their sections.

Tuning is the most common exercise in listening, and listening is the essence of music making. When the group tunes, it can be treated in an ordinary manner, or it can be expanded into games that impact ensemble awareness. There is no practical difference between a tuning reference note and a drone. Since improvising over a drone is a safe way to begin improvisational explorations, there is an opportunity to improvise every time the group tunes their instruments to a common tone.

Tuning Game 1. "Curved Air"

An oboist (or any wind or string player) uses their embouchure to "bend" the reference note a few cents sharp or flat. The rest of the group has to match the bent note in as exact unison as possible. The reference note bending can also be done by a string instrument. The purpose of this activity is to increase awareness of small differences in intonation, and to practice following a common intonation as an ensemble. The group is shadowing the person providing the reference tone.

Tuning Game 2. "Huff and Puff"

The oboist (or any wind or string player) uses body language to get the group to start the reference note together, all at once. The oboist also uses body language to conduct staccato "hits" in unison on the reference note. The purpose of this activity is to practice both common intonation and coordinated timing. Articulating notes together makes the group sound more crisp and energetic. When the players use visual cues to signal starting and stopping points, they are focusing on their peers instead of the printed page.

Tuning Game 3. Sah – rising, falling and rubbing

The conductor indicates with his or her hands to start the reference note together. Once started, the conductor puts his or her hands out front with one hand on top of the other. When the top hand slowly raises, the group slowly raises their note up a half step, bending gradually through the microtonal space. When the conductor's top hand slowly returns to rest on the bottom hand, the group slowly bends their note down a half step to the original starting note. For "Sah-falling," the conductor drops the bottom hand slowly, while the group slowly bends their note down a half step. For "Sah – rubbing," half the group is instructed to hold the original note and leave it as an unchanging drone. The other half of the group is conducted through Sah rising and Sah falling. The group hears the tension and release of the interval of a minor second as the notes bend up a half step or down a half step and back to the starting place. Once you divide the group in half, be sure to repeat the activity and have the two halves switch roles. As an extension of this activity, soloists can be invited to explore long tones and melodic phrases over the drone.

Tuning Game 4. "the Wave"

Instead of having all the instruments play the reference note simultaneously, the conductor indicates which players are active, sweeping the cue to play across the orchestra in whatever patterns he or she chooses. Players start and stop their notes as the gesture passes them by, much as a wave of raised hands passes through a stadium. This can be done playfully, with changes in the speed and the direction of the gestures. The overall effect is spatial, as the sound weaves through the ensemble. In this activity, the group is practicing intonation, timing, and following the conductor's visual signals. As an extension, one or more designated soloists can improvise as the sound moves from section to section or from row to row.

Tuning Game 5. "the Splash" (also called One Quality Sound)

On cue, each section leader plays and holds a randomly chosen note, with full commitment and responsiveness to the level of energy requested by the conductor's body language. What results is a tone cluster of as many notes as there are sections. The conductor ends the sounds, then conducts a new cluster with new body language. The group is instructed not to change their notes to sweeten the blending or avoid dissonance. Dissonance is part of the listening elements of the game. Expand the game by having each section mirror the note chosen by the section leader, and by having each player in the section take a turn initiating the note. Invite soloists to improvise over the tone clusters. Invite section leaders to improvise together in a free manner after playing five to six "Splashes" of sound.

Layered groove – a rhythm pattern activity for chorus

To prepare for this game, the leader models simple improvised phrases. Start a phrase as a call for the group to echo back. Once the group is echoing back the call accurately, establish a rhythm so the call can be repeated as a loop. The leader for this activity can be a teacher or a student once the structure of the game is established. This form is common in Bobby McFerrin's vocal workshops. If you adapt this activity for instruments, be sure to use phrases that are simple enough to copy easily.

To introduce the idea of a loop (a repeated part that follows a predictable pulse), set up a pulse using body percussion; for example, tap a pulse on your lap. While tapping the pulse as a group, give a call for call and response. The group will echo the call. Introduce a hand signal for "continue to play" (e.g.- rolling the hands). Turn one of the calls into a loop. Next introduce Sculpting. Designate a hand signal for dividing the group into sections like cutting a pizza (e.g.- chop your hands up and down while pointing to the seats where the section begins and ends). Designate one section of the group to continue the looped phrase (sculpt and signal "continue to play"). Stop the rest of the group. With the looped phrase as background, give a few new calls for call and response. This takes place while the first loop is being repeated by the section you sculpted. Turn one of these new calls into a second loop. Use sculpting to designate a section of the group to continue the second looped phrase. Now there will be two loops repeating. Stop the rest of the group. Repeat the process until there are four interleaved looped phrases going simultaneously. Request volunteer soloists and adjust the volume level of the group as needed. Bring the group volume down. Request volunteers to come up with new phrases for use as looped phrases. Assist the volunteers and edit their phrases, with consent, to make them workable. Continue changing the component phrases until there are four new parts. Each new phrase that becomes a call is the result of an improvised inspiration.

Use what they give you

If any singer comes up with a very catchy melody when improvising, ask them to repeat it and teach it to the group. This illustrates how improvising can lead to composing. Divide the group in three sections. One section holds a drone note. The second section sings the melody that came from one of the students. The third section "noodles," or improvises freely.

Chorus – incorporating drones as a support for improvisation

It is common for choruses to warm up by singing scales. Add an improvisation component to the warmup by adding a drone source, then singing the same scales over a drone. For variety, have some of the group, either volunteer soloists or whole sections, sing freely improvised melodies over a drone. Create a drone by playing fifths in the lower octaves of the piano while using the sustain pedal or use an organ or electronic shruti box if one is available. In the absence of instruments, part of the chorus can be recruited to hold a drone note.

If you warm up your chorus by singing scales and arpeggios, add an improvisational element in two steps. First, add a drone note. Assign the drone to half of your group while the other half sings scales. Switch the group roles so everyone has a turn holding a drone note. Next, divide the group so that half holds a drone and the other half "noodles," or improvises freely. Then switch which group is droning and which is improvising. Calling it "noodling" takes away some of the pressure to be a perfect performer. Improvising as a group allows the explorations to be anonymous, and thereby a bit safer. For advanced groups, add layers of harmony to the drone, including full chords with jazz extensions and suspensions. This will encourage improvising in a variety of tonal contexts.

Chorus - small ensemble activity

Request eight volunteers (plus a beat boxer/vocal percussion, if available). Set up a "song form" layered groove as follows: Two singers start a bass pattern that is repeated as a loop. Two singers add a complimentary rhythmic melodic pattern as a second loop, and if possible, they can harmonize their new part. Two additional singers add a third rhythmic melody, with harmony if possible, that fills the holes in the rhythms of the bass line and first loop. The last two singers solo or create improvised melody lines as an alternating conversation.

Activities for band – brass, woodwinds, percussion

Use the model for the Layered Groove chorus activity above but simplify the phrases to adjust for the instrumentalists' ability to imitate and match each other. In its simplest version, start with percussive phrases, or have all of the instruments play staccato on one note each. Create layered rhythmic grooves. Then invite instrumental soloists, using long tones or staccato tones. Lastly, invite instrumental soloists to improvise with no constraints.

Create a layered groove by section

Appoint a section leader for each section – trumpet, saxophone, trombone, clarinet, flute, baritone, pitched percussion, drums. The section leaders take turns adding a repeating loop part to a layered piece. The goal is for all of the players in the section to exactly match their section leader's part. Therefore, the part has to be clear and simple enough for the least skilled player in the section to "get it."

Band and Orchestra

Chromatic practice – "smooth lines" for sirening and "all in a row" for chromatic practice

Start with concert A, or with the note you use for tuning the brass instruments. Divide the group in half. One section holds the tuning note as a drone. The other half is free to explore, but they have to explore chromatically, all in adjacent half steps. They can go fast or slow, play in any rhythm, but the "game" is to keep their notes "all in a row." Switch which group is holding the drone note and which is chromatically exploring.

For strings and for instruments capable of continuously bending notes, the activity can be done in chromatic steps as above, or it can be done with continuous changes in pitch, like a siren.

In place of chromatic playing, a siren uses all of the space between one diatonic note and the next. Half the group holds the drone and half explores using sirening. They can go fast or slow, play in any rhythm, but the "game" is "smooth lines." Switch which group is holding the drone note and which is exploring.

Section variations

Have one section at a time explore over a drone that is held by all of the other sections. For example, flutes explore while the rest of the band holds a drone note. Be sure to include percussion in the activity. Drone notes are "held" by rolling on the xylophone, marimba, or bells. A piano can "hold" by rolling or by using the sustain pedal.

Play your instrument like a drum

Take a segment of a piece that you are working on as an ensemble. Play 8-16 measures. Have one section "lay out" and just listen. Then repeat that segment, and have the section that was listening join in, playing only percussive sounds on their instruments. This will highlight the rhythmic articulation of the piece. Start again using just the percussive sounds. The students will audiate the melodic aspects of the rhythms they are playing. Invite the remaining sections to join in, also using only percussive sounds. For the percussion instruments, have them play their stands and hardware, to be sure they are playing the rhythms in a new way. To add an improvisational component, have one section repeat the rhythmic core of a piece of music using only percussive sounds, while another section improvises over this repeated rhythm. The improvisation can be rhythmic or melodic.

Pizz and Strum for Orchestra

As a first step, have all players put their bows down. Each of the string instruments can play a two-finger chord using a combination of fingered and open strings. For the violins, they can finger an A on the low G string and an E on the D string. The result is fifths – AEAE. Since this is neither major nor minor, it supports improvisation in nearly any scale. This is what rock players call "power chords." For the violas and cellos, the analogous fingering includes a D on the low C string and an A on the adjacent G string, resulting in DADA.

Designate a section to be the "strummers." For example, let's start with the violas. Using an up and down motion of the thumb, the players strum a repeating rhythm: Down, down, down, down-up (or any rhythm that can be easily modeled). The violas strum in unison. The other sections "noodle" over the strumming, using only pizzicato sounds. Switch which section are the "strummers" and which are the improvisers. If the group is adept, allow bowed melodic improvising as well as pizzicato. Experiment with chromatic improvising and sirening as described above.

Coyote games

The "coyote" is the trickster. The coyote tries to get players to lose their rhythm home base or to drift from being in tune to being lost.

Have one section of your group hold a drone note. Designate one player in advance as the "coyote." That player tries to influence the section to play out of unison or out of tune. The section's job is to stick together and resist that influence. The group will learn to fine tune their listening to focus on their own section and filter out competing sounds. The coyote will learn how to identify who among the group is most prone to being influenced and will also learn whether playing something extremely different from the group or something nearly identical will give the coyote more power to influence others.

In the rhythmic version, have a section hold a repeated rhythm, either purely percussive or melodic. The designated "coyote" tries to influence the section to play out of time. The section's job is to stick together and resist that influence.

Teaching Contrast Using Group Size – the 54321 game

This game is meant for an ensemble that can improvise freely with each other. They will likely need reminders to use group size as a musical element in their improvising. This game provides practice in self-regulating the number of active players and thereby creating contrasts in their sound.

The idea is for the group to self-adjust so that the number of active players matches the number of fingers that the facilitator holds up. In a group of 25 for example, the leader might hold up 3 fingers. All but three players are supposed to drop out, but the leader does not indicate which three are to keep playing. The group has to pay close enough attention to its members to accomplish this task. This is not the most musical way of paring down, of course, since the emphasis at first is more visual (who is still playing) than auditory (what are the three remaining people playing). But it does introduce the dynamic of changing the number of active players to make artful contrasts in the overall sound. As the game continues, the leader holds up various numbers of fingers - any number from 10 to zero. One finger requires a single player to play alone. Zero means everyone is silent. Seven requires the group to look at each other and adjust until only seven players are active - a kind of musical chairs. And a skillful leader will make sure that the game includes many segments in which everyone is playing. It would be worthwhile to notice how much the whole group's improvising changes after they have experienced the smaller group's sounds.

Part Ten - Bibliography

Darling, David and Weber, Julie. The Darling Conversations. Manifest Spirit Music, 2007.

Faulkner, Simon. Rhythm to Recovery. Philadelphia: Jessica Kingsley, 2016.

Green, Barry. Bringing Music to Life. Chicago: GIA Publications, 2009.

Hale, Susan Elizabeth. Song and Silence. Albuquerque: La Alameda Press, 1995.

Hull, Arthur. Drum Circle Facilitation. Santa Cruz: Village Music Circles, 2006.

Knysh, Mary and Bevan, Betsy. BoomDoPa. Bloomsburg: Rhythmic Connections, 2000.

Knysh, Mary. Innovative Drum Circles: Beyond Beat into Harmony. Millville: Rhythmic Connections, 2013.

Lieberman, Julie Lyonn. Planet Musician. Milwaukee: Hal Leonard, 1998.

Mathieu, Allaudin. The Listening Book. Boston:Shambala, 1991.

Miller, Lynn. SpiritArts – Transformation Through Creating Art, Music and Dance. Phoenixville: Expressive Therapy Press, 2013.

Nachmanovitch, Stephen. Free Play. New York: Tarcher/Putnam, 1991.

Oliveros, Pauline. Deep Listening: A Composer's Sound Practice. New York: iUniverse, Inc., 2005.

Oshinsky, James. Return to Child. Goshen: Music for People, 2008.

Oshinsky, James. Music Doctor Improv Cards and Picture Prompts. Self-published, 2021.

Rhiannon. Vocal River: The Skill and Spirit of Improvisation. Hawaii:Rhiannon Music, 2013.

Rhiannon. Flight (Interactive Guide to Vocal Improvisation). Boulder: Sounds True, 2000.

Sobol, Elise. An Attitude and Approach for Teaching Music to Special Learners. Lanham: Rowman and Littlefield Education, 2008.

Treece, Roger. Circlesongs - The Method. Rogertreece.com/books-scores, 2015.

Wooten, Victor. The Music Lesson. New York: Berkley Books, 2006.

Annotated Bibliography

Wooten, Victor. The Music Lesson. New York: Berkley Books, 2006.
This may be the best book on musicianship I have ever come across. In the style of Carlos Castaneda, the device of this book involves an ordinary working jazz/rock bass player is visited by characters with supernatural powers that they instruct him in. These abilities have to do with the fundamentals of music, from time and pace to tone and ensemble awareness. They are taught through experiences in nature and in honing mindfulness, which makes this a book about personal as well as musical development. It is a very engaging read.

Mathieu, Allaudin. The Listening Book. Boston: Shambala, 1991.
Mathieu, a composer and author of Harmonic Experience, suggests a variety of activities and practices for refining one's listening as a path to deeper personal engagement in music. This is the kind of book where you can open to any page randomly and find a gem.

Hull, Arthur. Drum Circle Facilitation. Santa Cruz: Village Music Circles, 2006.
No one has done more than Hull in the area of articulating the mindset needed to conduct large group rhythm experiences, from classrooms to arenas. His book is filled with personal anecdotes of his successes and train wrecks, and his codification of rhythm activities and leadership skills is comprehensive and clear.

Hull, Arthur. Rhythmic Alchemy Playshop Volume #1: Drum Circle Games. Santa Cruz: Village Music Circles, 2013. This book contains the group games Hull most often uses in his workshops, along with a DVD for illustrating how to lead them. The three types of games are Agreement games, with preset rules; Facilitated games, where a leader interacts or directs during the game, and Orchestration games, where the leadership role shifts from person to person during the game.

Green, Barry. Bringing Music to Life. Chicago: GIA Publications, 2009.
A classical bassist and author of The Inner Game of Music, in this book Green talks about his own path to improvisation through the teachings of cellist David Darling and the organization Music for People.

Oshinsky, James. Return to Child: Music for People's Guide to Improvising Music and Authentic Group Leadership. Goshen: Music for People, 2008.
Teaching improvisation can be approached as an improvisation. The skills for participating in solo, small ensemble and large group improvisations are presented in the first chapters, with specific mention of instrument categories (strings, piano, drums) and musical styles. The middle chapters address the mindset of the leader and the common challenges of teaching improvisation to mixed groups. The final section of the book covers ways of bringing improvisation into classrooms.

Oshinsky, James. Music Doctor Improv Cards and Picture Prompts. Self-published, 2021.
A set of 54 cards containing the roles people can fulfill in small group improvisation. Divided into four "suits," improvisation basics, support roles, incorporating current and historical musical styles, and uses of contrast and silence. Each card has a different picture on its reverse side to inspire soundtrack-type improvisations in various moods. An accompanying booklet has suggestions for using each card in music education settings.

Knysh, Mary and Bevan, Betsy. BoomDoPa. Bloomsburg: Rhythmic Connections, 2000.
A book of improvisation-based rhythm games for the school music classroom. It emphasizes hand drum techniques and the use of plastic Boomwhackers.

Knysh, Mary. Innovative Drum Circles: Beyond Beat into Harmony. Millville: Rhythmic Connections, 2013. A book of improvisation-based activities for school music classrooms and adult workshops. It is truly innovative. The activities transition from rhythm-only to rhythmic melodic and rhythmic harmonic skills. This is a way to build more layers of musicianship while keeping the accessibility of rhythm as a starting point for group improvisation.

Lieberman, Julie Lyonn. Planet Musician. Milwaukee: Hal Leonard, 1998.
Violinist Lieberman describes how to capture the essence of a variety of world music styles.
Hale, Susan Elizabeth. Song and Silence. Albuquerque: La Alameda Press, 1995.
A book about the uses of the voice in music therapy, personal expression, and musical performance.

Sobol, Elise. An Attitude and Approach for Teaching Music to Special Learners. Lanham: Rowman and Littlefield Education, 2008. The title is very descriptive. The author is a strong advocate for addressing the needs of Special Education students in mainstream school settings and is an excellent trainer of teachers.

Rhiannon. Flight (Interactive Guide to Vocal Improvisation). Boulder: Sounds True, 2000. Rhiannon (no last name) is a long-time member of Bobby McFerrin's performing ensemble. This 2 CD set is a music-minus-one class in vocal improvisation that invites you to sing along and make up your own parts to the ensemble's vocal grooves.

Rhiannon. Vocal River: The Skill and Spirit of Improvisation. Hawaii:Rhiannon Music, 2013. This book has Rhiannon's biography as well as the vocal activities she most often uses in her jazz-oriented vocal improvisation workshops.

Darling, David and Weber, Julie. The Darling Conversations. Manifest Spirit Music, 2007. Cellist David Darling and educator/composer Julie Weber discuss a humanistic approach to music improvisation that encourages the musical impulse in all people and expresses a philosophy that all combinations of people, instruments, and experience levels can make music together. The 3 CD set contains numerous examples of small ensemble improvisation techniques, based on Darling's work with the organization, Music for People.

Faulkner, Simon. Rhythm to Recovery. Philadelphia: Jessica Kingsley, 2016. Simon Faulkner is a pioneer in using drum circle activities to promote pro-social awareness and actions in at-risk populations such as delinquent youth and incarcerated adults. His work, sponsored by the government of Australia, is meticulously researched and verified. The activities are accessible and practical, fun, and engaging. The therapeutic metaphors that accompany the activities are brilliant.

Treece, Roger. Circlesongs – The Method. This is the method for group vocal improvisation taught at the workshops of Bobby McFerrin and his colleagues. The book contains three audio CDs with examples of vocal improv exercises and circlesongs created by Mr. Treece and his workshop attendees.

Miller, Lynn. SpiritArts. Lynn is a long-time colleague of David Darling and is adept at describing his vocal and instrumental improvisation activities. But she is also a dancer, a visual artist and a shamanic healer. Her book integrates the various improvisational modalities for the purpose of personal transformation and healing.

Oliveros, Pauline. Deep Listening: A Composer's Sound Practice. New York: iUniverse, Inc., 2005. Deep Listening, as developed by Pauline Oliveros, explores the difference between the involuntary nature of hearing and the voluntary, selective nature of listening. The practice includes bodywork, sonic meditations, and interactive performance, as well as listening to the sounds of daily life, nature, one's own thoughts, imagination, and dreams. It cultivates a heightened awareness of the sonic environment, both external and internal, and promotes experimentation, improvisation, collaboration, playfulness, and other creative skills vital to personal and community growth. (Deep Listening website)

Nachmanovitch, Stephen. Free Play. New York: Tarcher/Putnam, 1991
The whole enterprise of improvisation in life and art, of recovering free play and awakening creativity, is about being true to ourselves and our visions. Free Play is about the inner sources of spontaneous creation, why we create and what we learn when we do. It integrates material from a wide variety of sources among the arts, sciences, and spiritual traditions of humanity. Filled with unusual quotes, amusing and illuminating anecdotes, and original metaphors, it reveals how inspiration arises within us, how that inspiration may be blocked, derailed or obscured by certain unavoidable facts of life, and how finally it can be liberated to speak or sing, write or paint, dance or play, with our own authentic voice. (Thrift Books review)

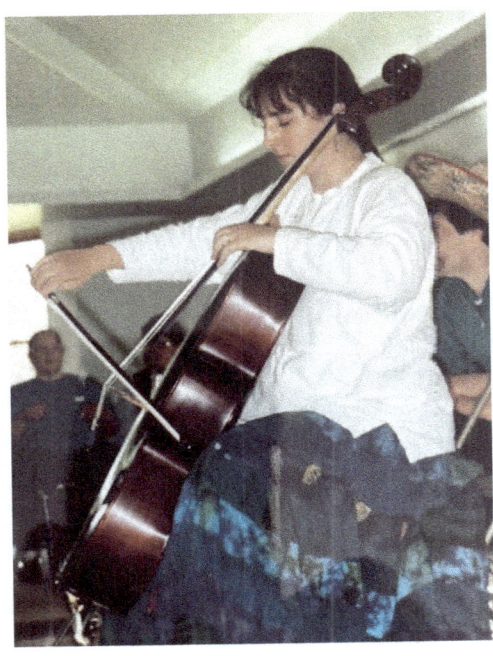

In memorium – Emily Metcalf and David Darling.

Appendix – Using Flash Cards as a Teaching Tool for Improvisation

The *Music Doctor Improv Cards and Picture Prompts* is a deck of flash cards. They identify a total of 54 roles that players can serve in a group improvisation, divided between four "suits" - improvisation basics, support roles, incorporating current and historical musical styles, and employing contrast and silence. The cards each have a different evocative picture on the back, so they can be used to inspire soundtrack improvisations. If you practice all these skills, you will develop depth and breadth in your improvising.   Included is a Teacher Activity Booklet that describes each skill, its importance and usefulness in improvising, and ways to present the skills in classroom and workshop settings.

The cards are available at the following websites: www.westmusic.com/530739   and www.tinyurl.com/Musicdr.

Some years ago, I pieced together a gizmo that has four document clips facing the four directions. It fits on a mic stand and will hold four of the flash cards, each facing a different member of a seated quartet. I put four cards in the holder and let the players read them briefly before starting an improvisation. The players see only their own card.

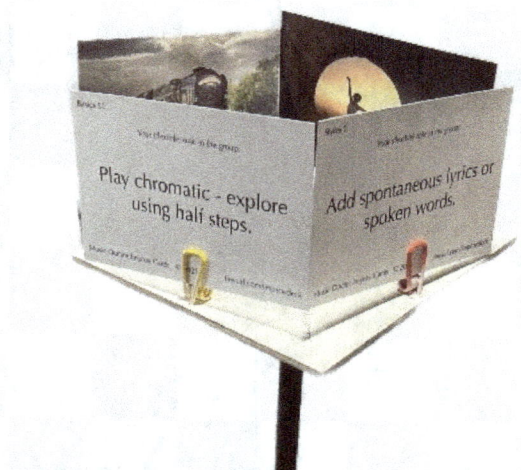

A flat board with clips installed and a 5/8 inch center hole fits most mic stands.

Preselecting card combinations

When using the cards for the first time in a class, I will preselect card combinations that I know will yield complementary roles among the players, and that will avoid putting players in student crisis mode (not knowing how to do something). Using the cards will quicken the process of learning the roles one can fill and will nudge players into trying the roles that they might not spontaneously think of. Here is an example of a workable set of cards for use early in an improvisation class:

1. ostinato - play a consistent groove
2. match pulse and create accents
3. play with full emotional power
4. hear what the group sounds like without you now and then

This combination has a rhythm section of ostinato and pulse, an emotional soloist, and a person who will emphasize space by dropping out. By rotating the card holder while the students are playing, they can experience all of the different roles.

Another basic combination:
1. drone - play one unchanging note
2. play your instrument in a new way
3. play long tones
4. offer a chord progression

This combination will yield harmonic contrasts as the chords change against an unchanging drone. The long tone player and the one playing in a new way will have the solo opportunities.

A third option:
1. play a descending scale
2. play a heartbeat rhythm
3. support the tonal center
4. ooh energy - rhapsody and lullaby

A true heartbeat rhythm (lub-dub-rest-lub-dub-rest, etc) is in a triple meter. A descending scale in triple meter leaves space for movement and pauses. This might set up a gentle piece in which ooh energy melodies will complement the rhythm.

In contrast, it is possible to set up a combination that will encourage the players to be more fiery and risky:
1. provide the drama
2. inspire your partners to get loud and move
3. use your instrument as a drum
4. add lyrics or spoken word

In this combination, all the suggestions are vague and abstract. With fewer constrictions there is more room for open expression.

It is worth noting that the roles on the cards are not commands. None of the players are restricted to playing only what the cards suggest. They are always free to interact and follow the music that is spontaneously occurring. In addition to the freedom that is built into the way the instructor presents the cards, it is often useful to give each quartet a segment of time in which they interact freely and play without regard to any outside suggestions.

Improvisation Basics

1. Sing what you play, Play what you sing
2. Ooh energy - rhapsody and lullaby
3. Yea! energy - strong calls for celebration or warning
4. Musical conversations with group partners
5. Shadowing - imitation in real time
6. Harmonize what a partner is playing
7. Match pulse and create accents
8. Ostinato - play a consistent groove
9. Use your instrument as a drum
10. Drone - play one unchanging note
11. Chromatic - explore using half steps
12. Do as much as you can with only one note
13. Play as many "wrong notes" as possible

Support Roles

1. Listen for flow, and don't play all the time
2. Play to bring the group together
3. Influence the group to play what you play
4. Imitate more than you initiate
5. Provide a groove
6. Offer a descending scale
7. Play bass
8. Play a heartbeat rhythm
9. Listen for who needs support
10. Offer a chord progression
11. Support the tonal center
12. Inspire others to support you
13. Play long tones

Contrast and Silence

1. Solo or be silent
2. Provide the drama
3. Be a disruptor
4. Play your instrument in a new way
5. Listen for the moment of greatest impact
6. Play in a different meter
7. Play with full emotional power
8. Play in odd numbered meters
9. Use 50 notes, then stop
10. Hear what the group is like without you
11. Enter, leave, re-enter, leave again
12. Emphasize silence and space
13. Be independent

Current and Historical Musical Styles

1. Add lyrics or spoken words
2. Play something you love to play
3. Pointillism - brief textural sparkles
4. Fugue - imitate and repeat your partners
5. Blues - play with soul
6. Minimalist - simplicity and small changes
7. Funk - make your partners want to dance
8. Country, folk, and bluegrass
9. Music of any culture or time period
10. Play something familiar extra slowly
11. Include a familiar melody or hook
12. Inspire your partners to get loud and move
13. Play soft until your partners join you

Jokers

1. Be the clown or the fool
2. Add an element of humor

Acknowledgements

Music for People began in the 1980s as the brainchild of cellist David Darling and flautist Bonnie Insull. Both musicians loved to improvise and to connect with players at all levels of musical experience. Darling invented many of the games we describe in these pages, and Insull saw these simple structures as entry points for creating an inclusive music making community in which there was no divide between players and audience.

In the early years of the organization a very diverse collection of like-minded musicians and educators gravitated to this way of improvising and collaborated on refinements, creating a corpus of activities and a style of teaching that flowed like a piece of music. Central to the approach was an attitude of acceptance and encouragement for everyone who dared to take the risk to play along.

The first workshops were held near David Darling's home in Connecticut, hosted in the barn of Joanie and Bill Spear. There was also a hub of improvisation activity in Princeton, NJ, anchored by Catherine Judd, Ange Chianese, and Jane Buttars. A cadre of improvisers emerged in Montreal, where Lise Roy, Josee Allard, Monique Poirier, and Chantal Drapeau brought their French-inspired sensitivities to the music.

The pioneering group that began Music for People included Emily Metcalf, a symphony cellist, Ken Guilmartin, a composer and educator who went on to found the preschool program Music Together, Paul Butler, a career woodwind musician and producer, and the authors of this work, Mary Knysh and James Oshinsky. They were soon joined by other talented and dedicated musicians and educators who brought tremendous diversity to the musical worlds that were represented, from avant-garde classical music to African drumming to folk, rock, and bluegrass. This work would not have developed without the teaching contributions of Julie Weber, Betsy Bevan, Lynn and Eric Miller, and Ron Kravitz and the production assistance of Bonnie Darling and Breanna Metcalf-Oshinsky.

Over the years, the depth of the work has been enhanced by the efforts of David Rudge, Jan Hittle, Eric Edberg, Rob Falvo, Joelle Danant, Irene Feher, Alina Plourde, Alison Weiner, Sarah Tenney, Thomasina Levy, Stuart Fuchs, Clint Goss, Julie Cook, Sara Swersey, Mark Hinkley, Sally Childs-Helton, Harold McKinney, Jonathan Best, Patrick Whitehead, Annie O'Shea, Alison Cardinet, Sadja Greenwood, Ted Zook, Kevin Makarewiscz and Sharon Little. Clíodhna Ní Aodáin, Alexander Merz, Bernhard Maurer, Michael Horowitz, Christof Weismann, Marisa Perez, and Matthias Rauh have helped spread this work in Europe. We apologize for any inadvertent omissions among these credits. Our community is large, international, and has survived the challenges of making live improvised music through a pandemic.

At the draft stage of this project, the careful eyes of Mary Knysh, Scott Edgar, Irene Feher, Harold McKinney, Tim Simmons, Leanne Darling, Carol Purdy, Sarah Tenney, JoAnn Spies and Martha Crowell helped shape the mass of observations and experiences into a coherent linear tale. Heather Daly gave permission to use her artwork for the cover, and Jill Carter helped design what you see.

Personally, I would not have been able to piece together this work without the support and discerning editing eye of my wife Mary, who knows the lyrics to every song, and who helps contain and focus the chaotic crosscurrents of my creative process.

The activities of Social Music Improvisation, and creative ways to present them in music classes, performing ensembles, and workshops, are described in detail in books and articles available from the authors (see Bibliography).

James Oshinsky   PsyDoctorO@optonline.net   www.tinyurl.com/musicdr

Mary Knysh   MaryKnysh@gmail.com   www.music4Wellness.com

Oshinsky, James with Knysh, Mary. Simple and Daring: Teaching Social Music Improvisation - Facilitation and Flow. Bundt Pan Publishing ©2023.

Oshinsky, James and Knysh, Mary. Original Art, Original Writing, Original Music – Making room for improvisation in school music. Article in preparation, ©2023.

Photo credits: Pixabay.com, Unsplash.com, Julie Weber, Sharon Little, Betsy Bevan, Mary Knysh, James Oshinsky

Cover art: Heather Daly "Celestial Grooves"   Design assistance: Jill Carter

"Music in Nature" Betsy Bevan

About the authors:

For over 30 years, Jim Oshinsky has been a musical adventurer, immersed in the teachings of great improvisers and master teachers - David Darling, Paul Winter, Victor Wooten, Bobby McFerrin, and Susan Osborn. He became an ambassador of a welcoming form of improvisation based on social and musical connections. As the Director of the Improvisation Ensemble at Adelphi University for over ten years, Jim prepared music teachers-to-be in the ways of improvisational music and flowing sequences of teaching. In this volume, Jim shares the resources he has gathered, beginning with the open attitude of the improviser and the facilitator to keep things simple and daring. Simple - in the words of the late David Darling, "to be a master of what you can control." Daring - to jump in, start something, and find your path in the spontaneous flow, whether you are teaching music or playing it. Jim is a Remo-endorsed educator and a licensed clinical psychologist.

Mary Knysh has been the lead teacher of Music for People and Rhythmic Connections for the past three decades, presenting brain-based programs for immersive music internationally. She is an award-winning trainer of music teachers, using the methods of flow and facilitation described in this book to craft deep learning experiences with seamless sequences of activities for children, adults, and elders. She is an endorser for Rhythm Band, Toca, and Peripole Music.

About the book:

Based on the pioneering improvisation workshops of the late cellist David Darling, *Simple and Daring* presents suggestions for teaching Social Music Improvisation to children and adults at all levels of ability and experience. There are specific ideas for incorporating improvisation into the common practices of band, orchestra, and chorus in schools. There are dozens of tried-and-true teaching sequences that provide entryways into the world of spontaneous music. And there is a crosswalk between the teaching of Social Music Improvisation and the main tenets of Social Emotional Learning: identity, belonging and agency. This approach to improvisation allows people to interact in socially beneficial ways while making artful, authentic, and connected spontaneous music that inspires rhythm and harmony in their lives.

A lot of preparation goes into being ready to be spontaneous. For musicians, we can become skilled improvisers if we have good models and ample experience, the way we learn to be fluent in a language. For teachers, we can use a parallel process – teaching improvisation with spontaneity – if we immerse ourselves in a supportive atmosphere to take risks and learn by doing. This book provides the path, which is both intentional and intuitive.